Whimsical Mandalas

Coloring Book for Adults

by Christea Blue

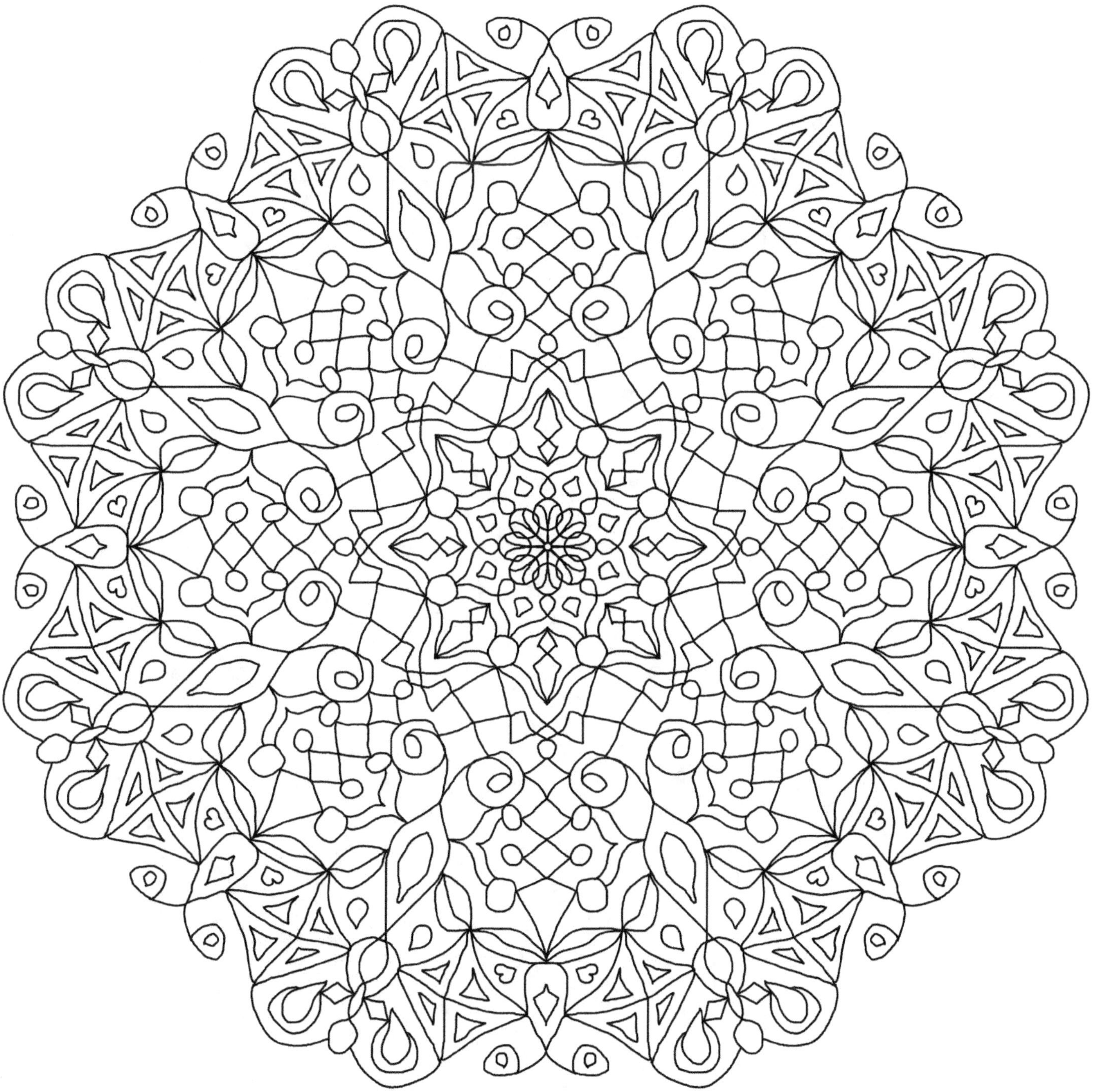

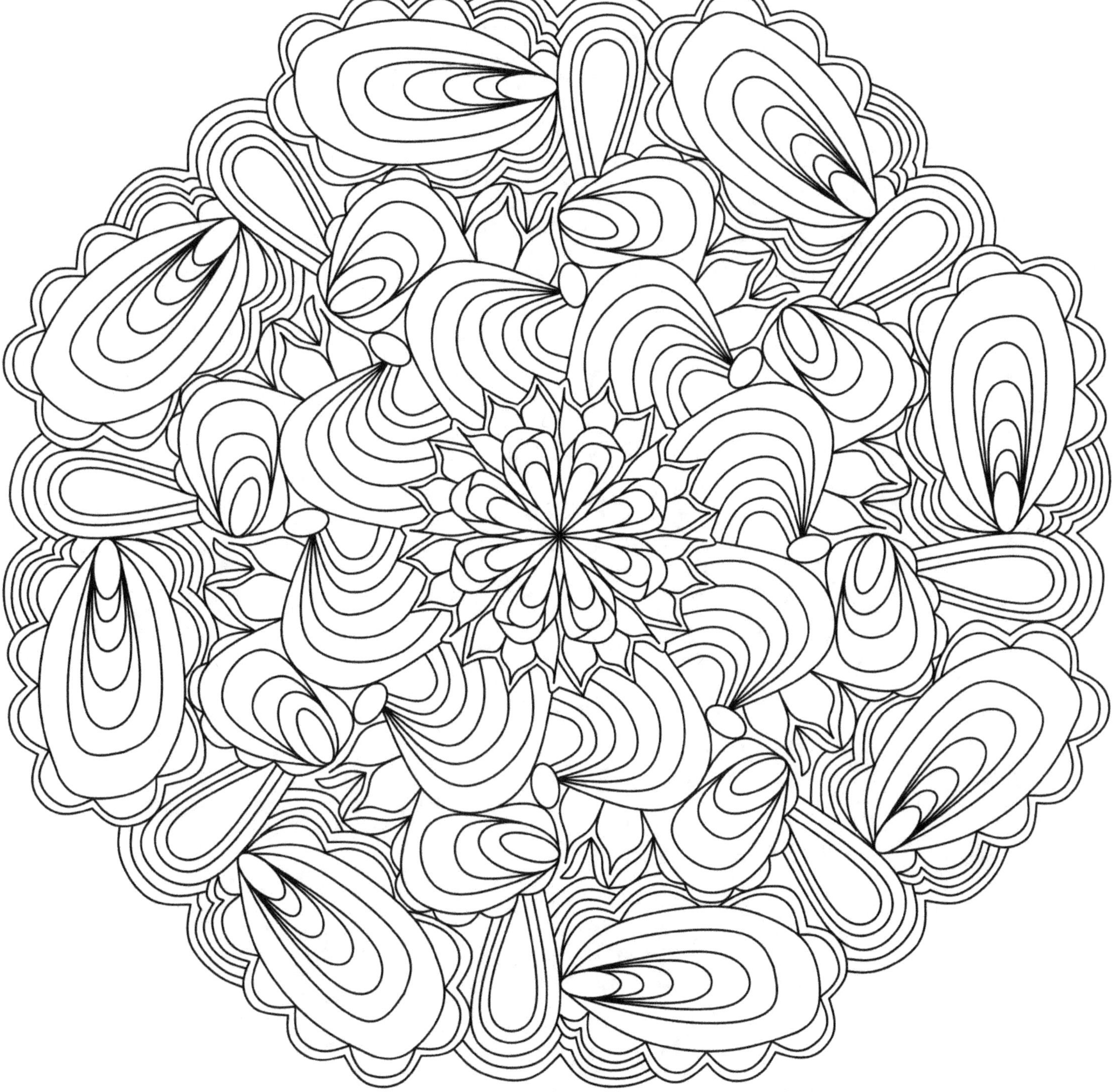

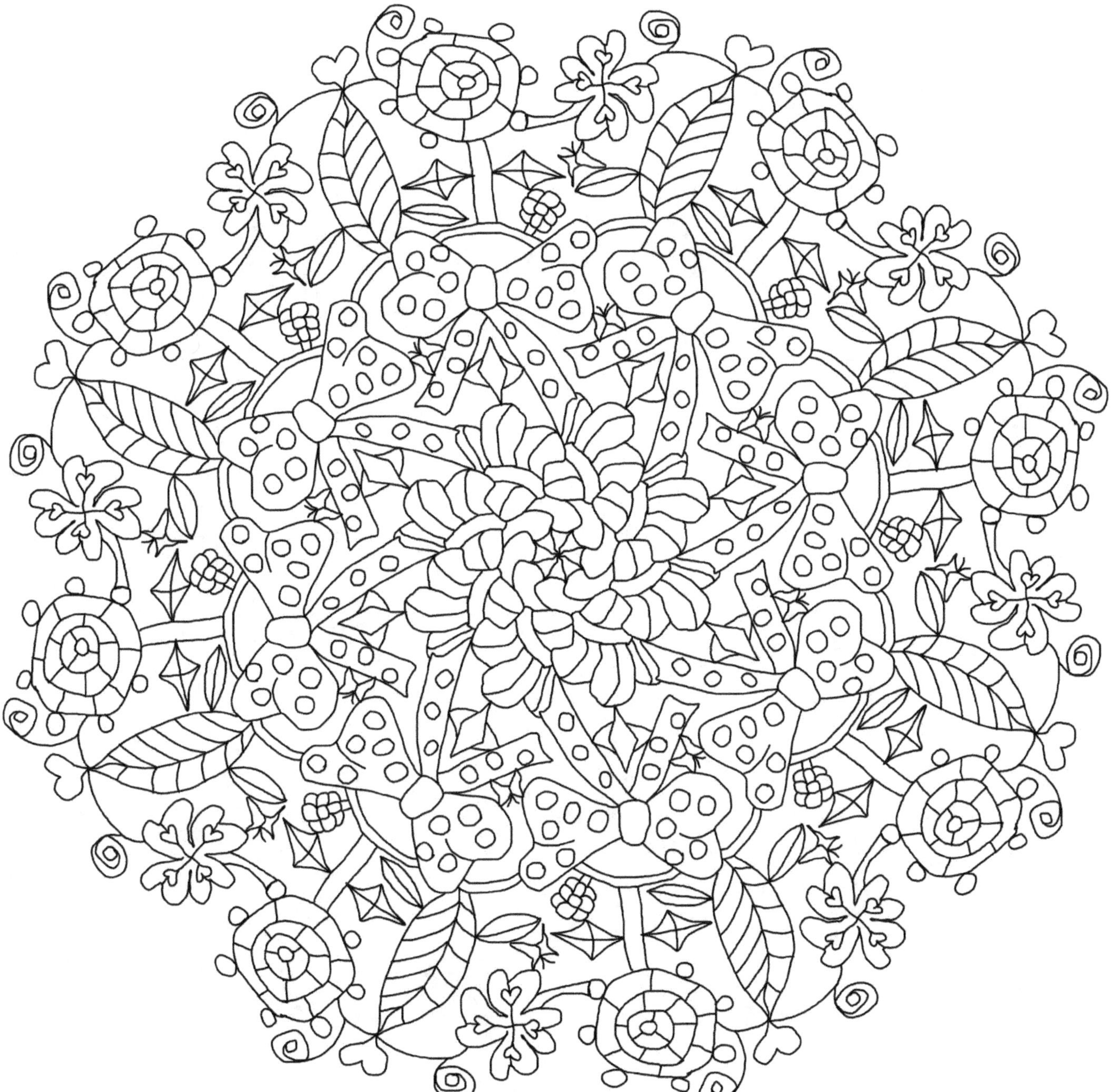

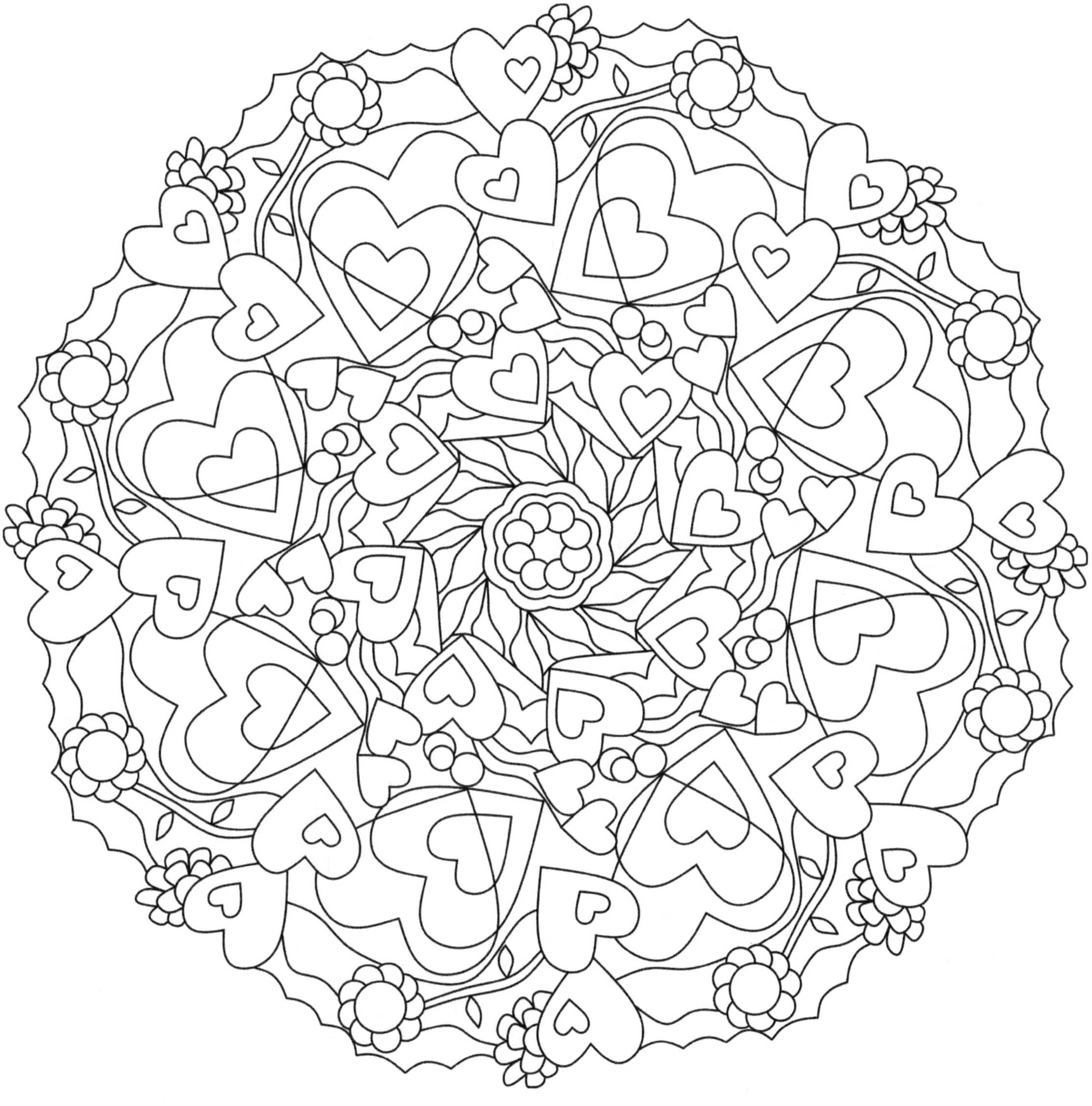

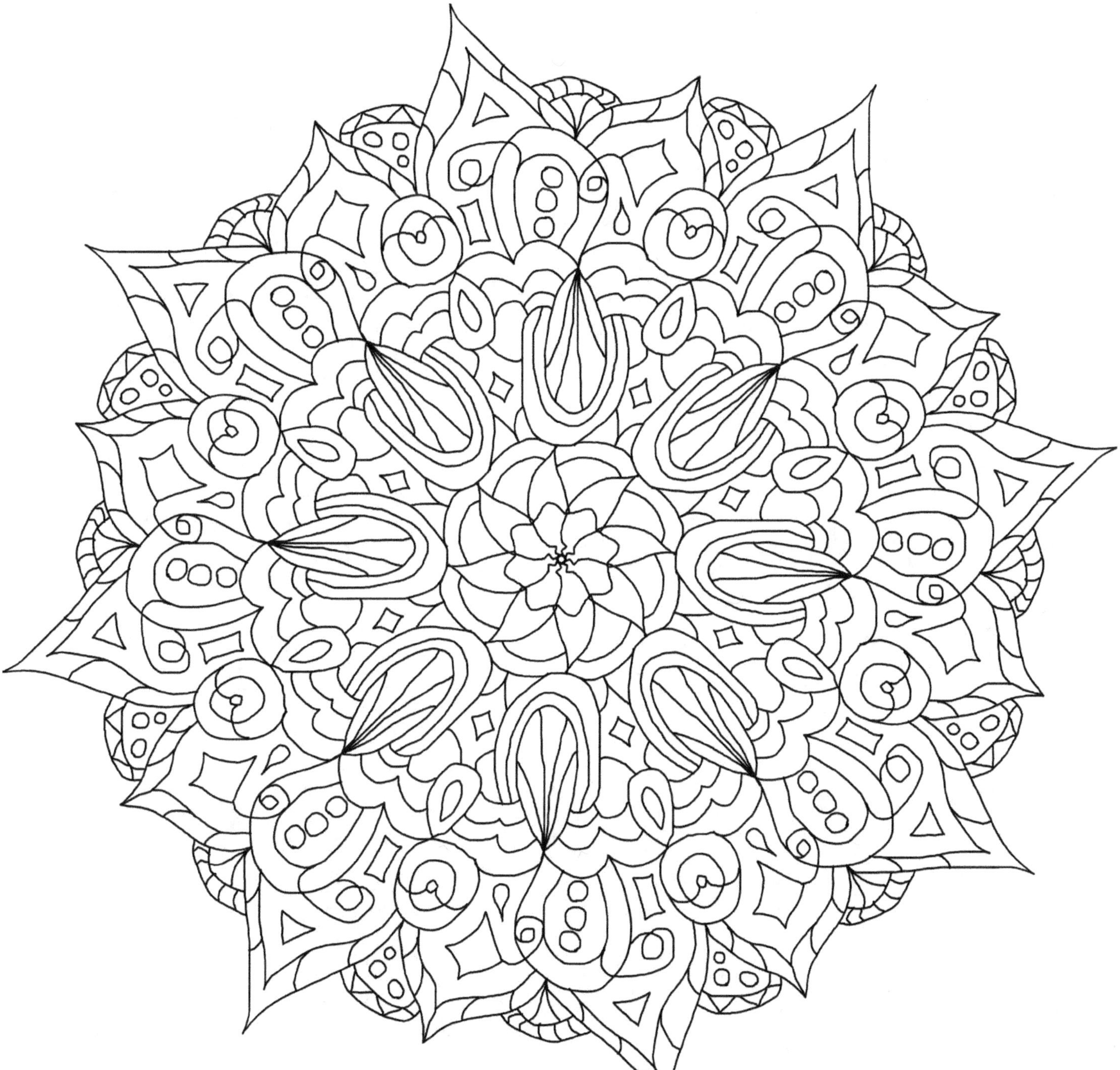

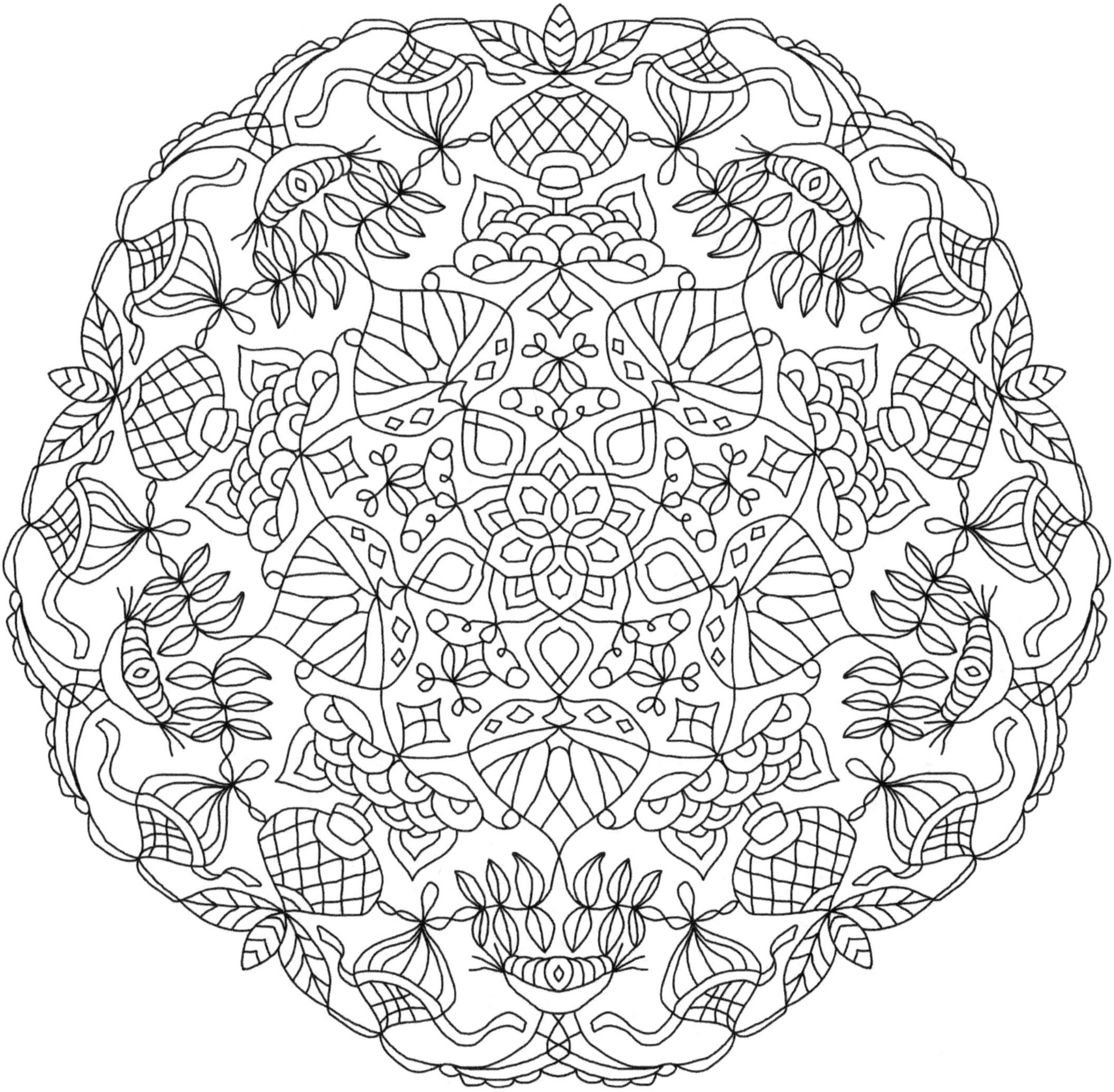

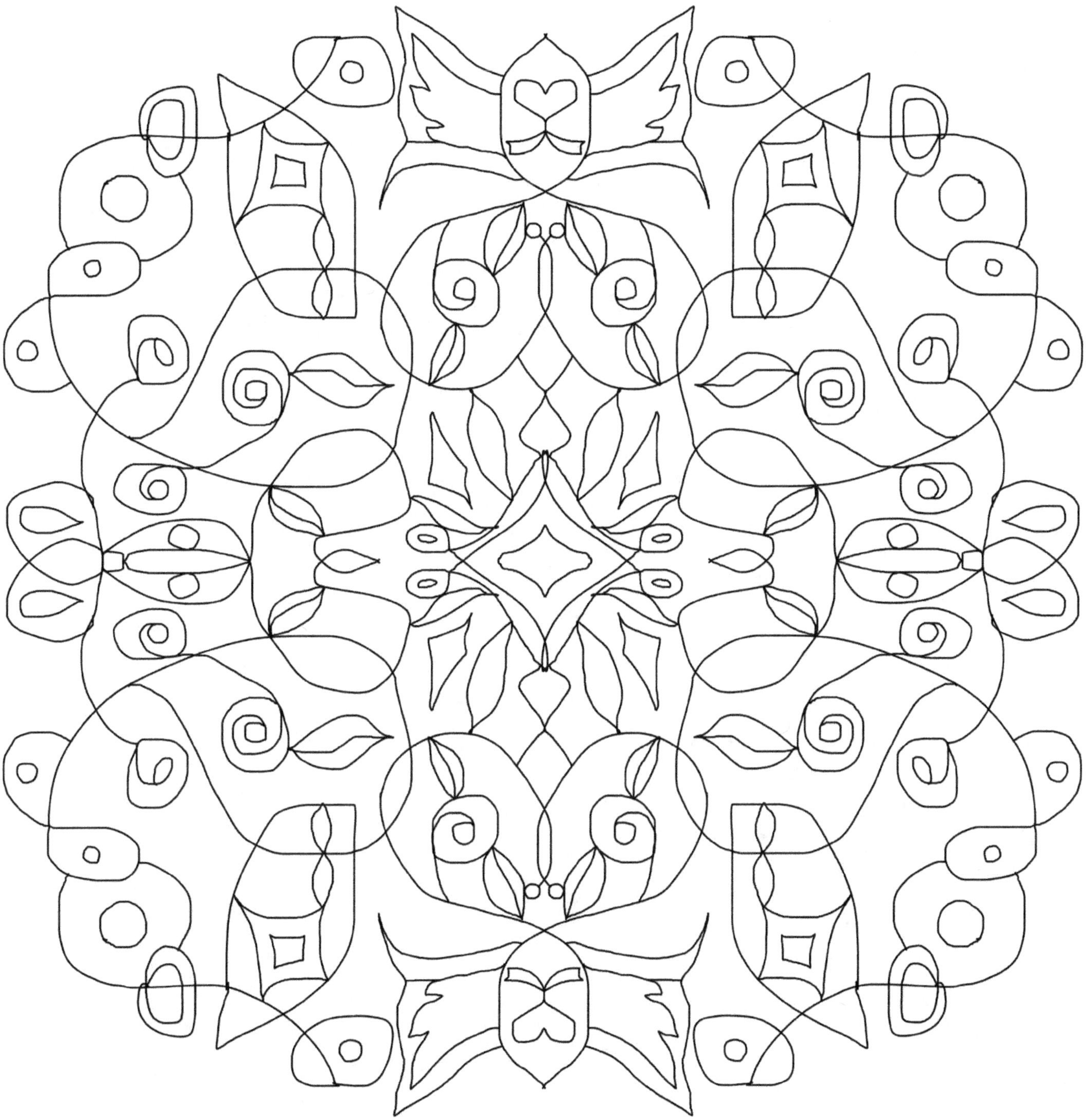

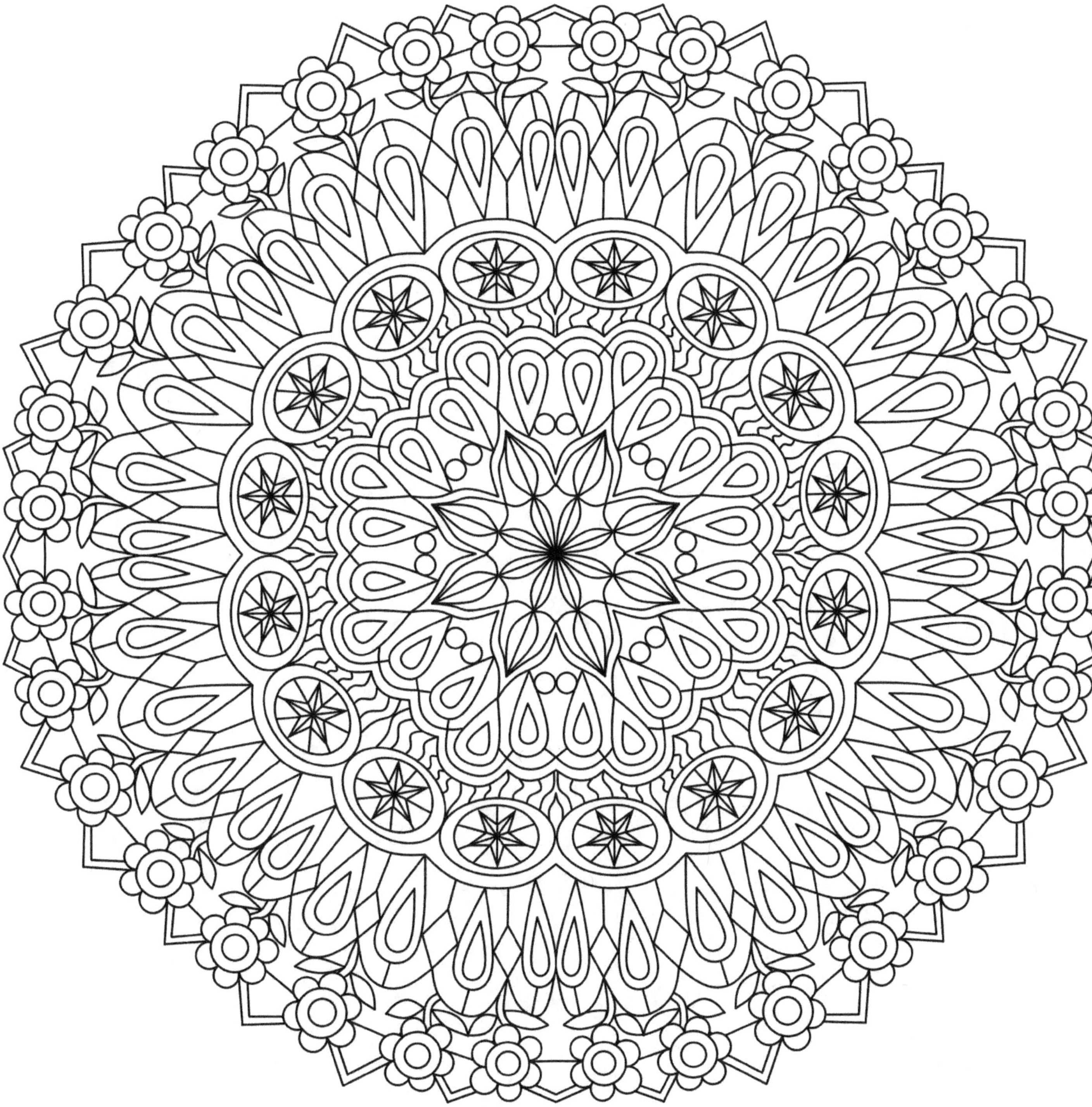

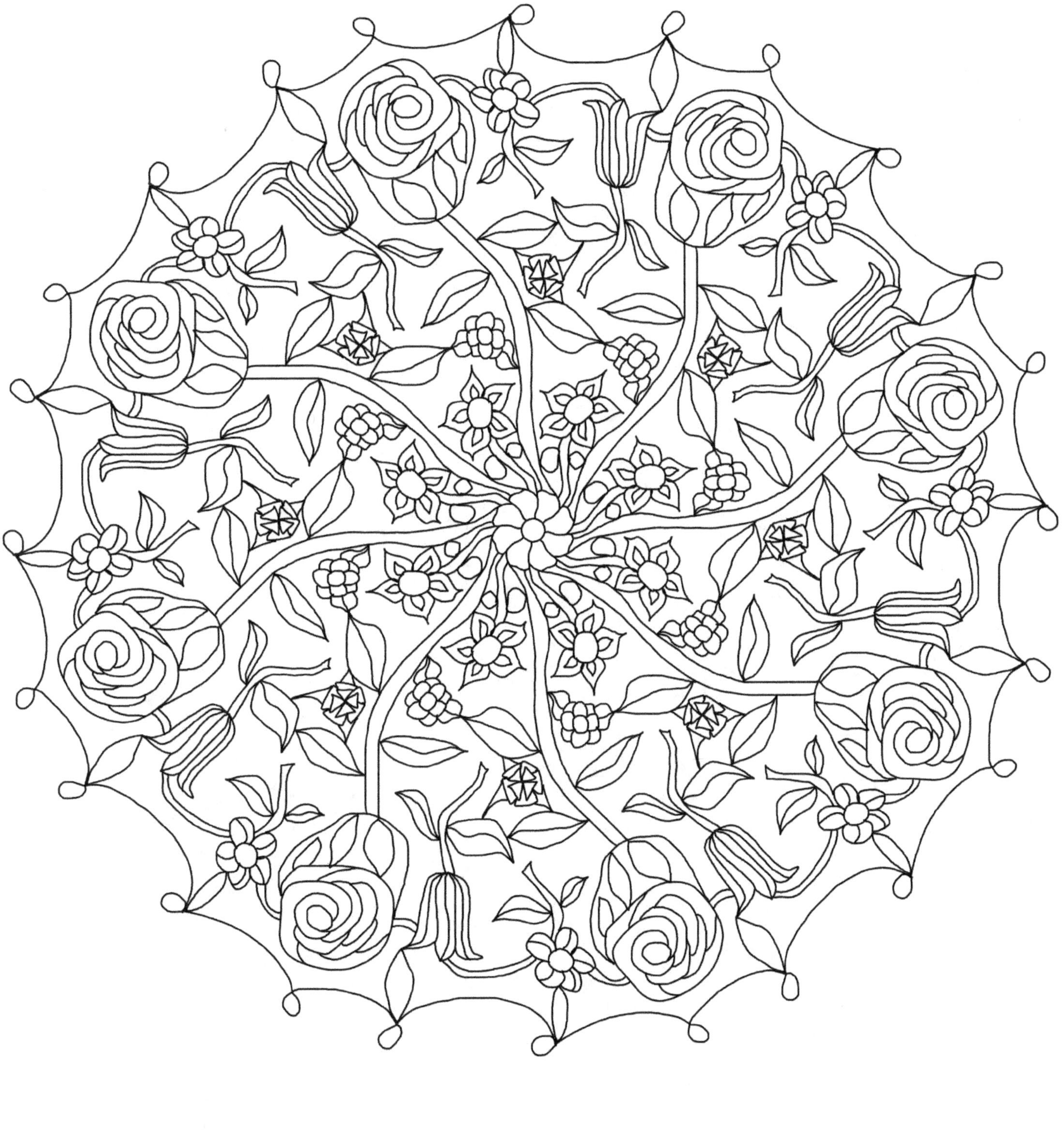

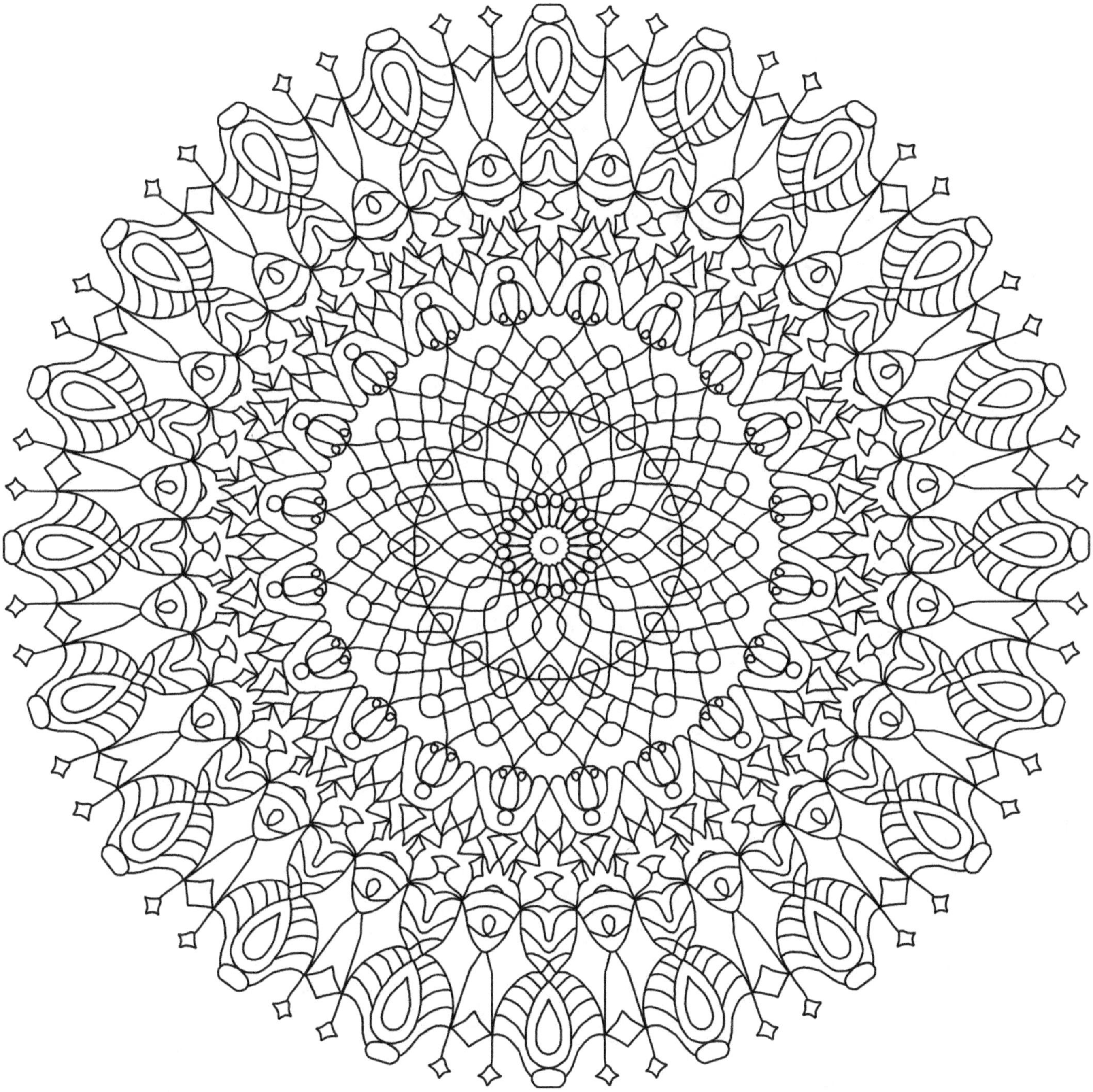

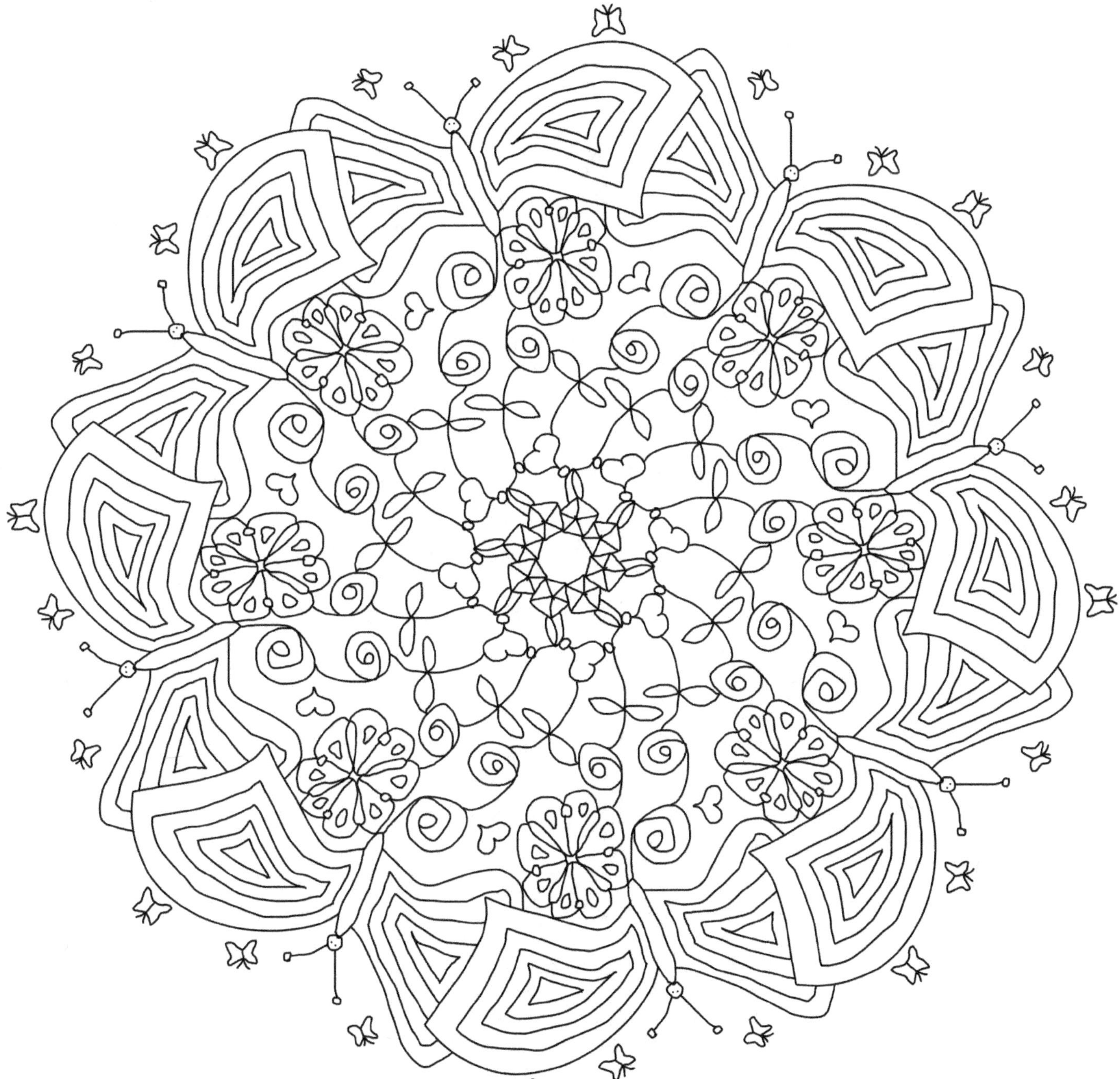

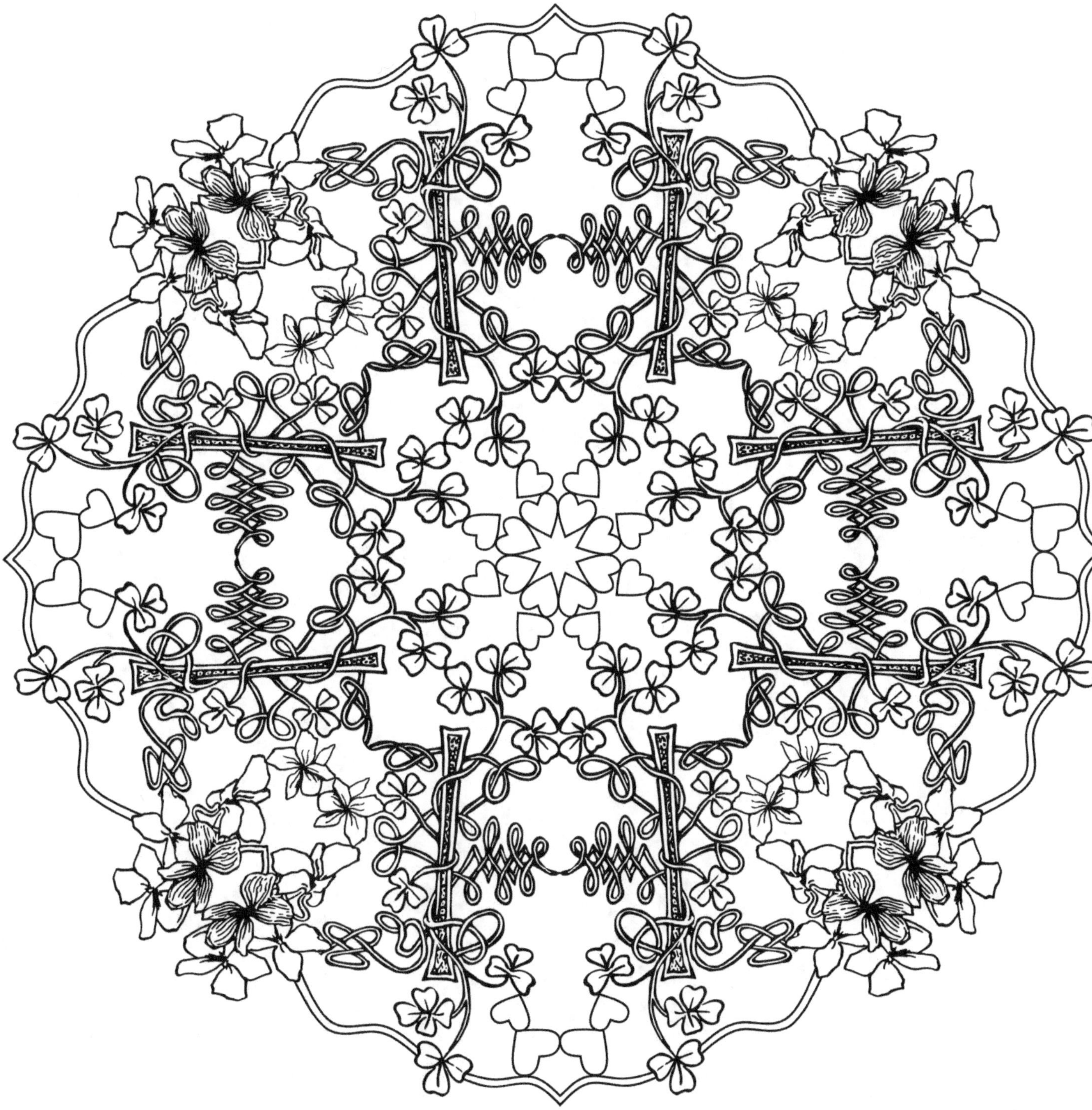

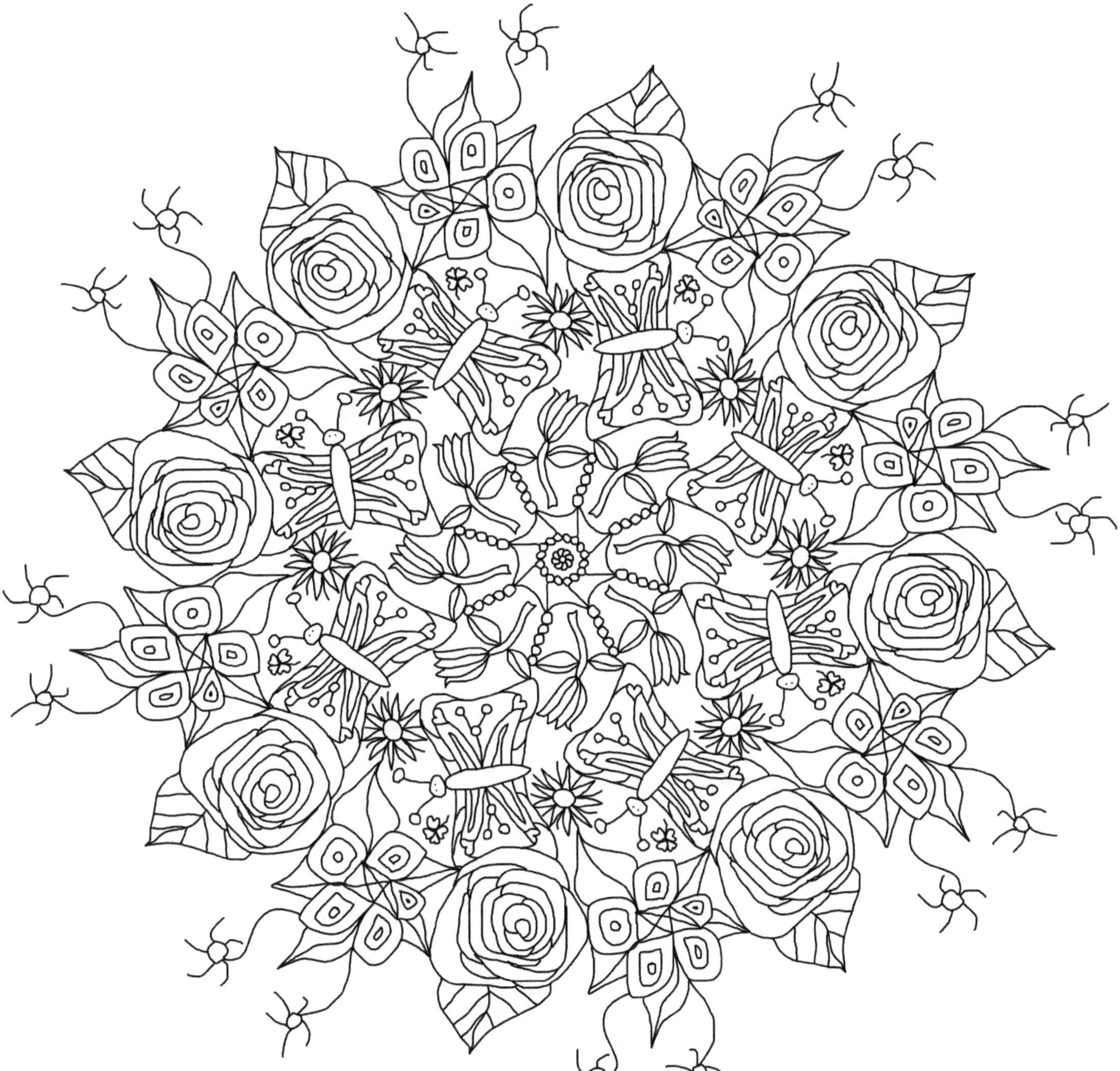

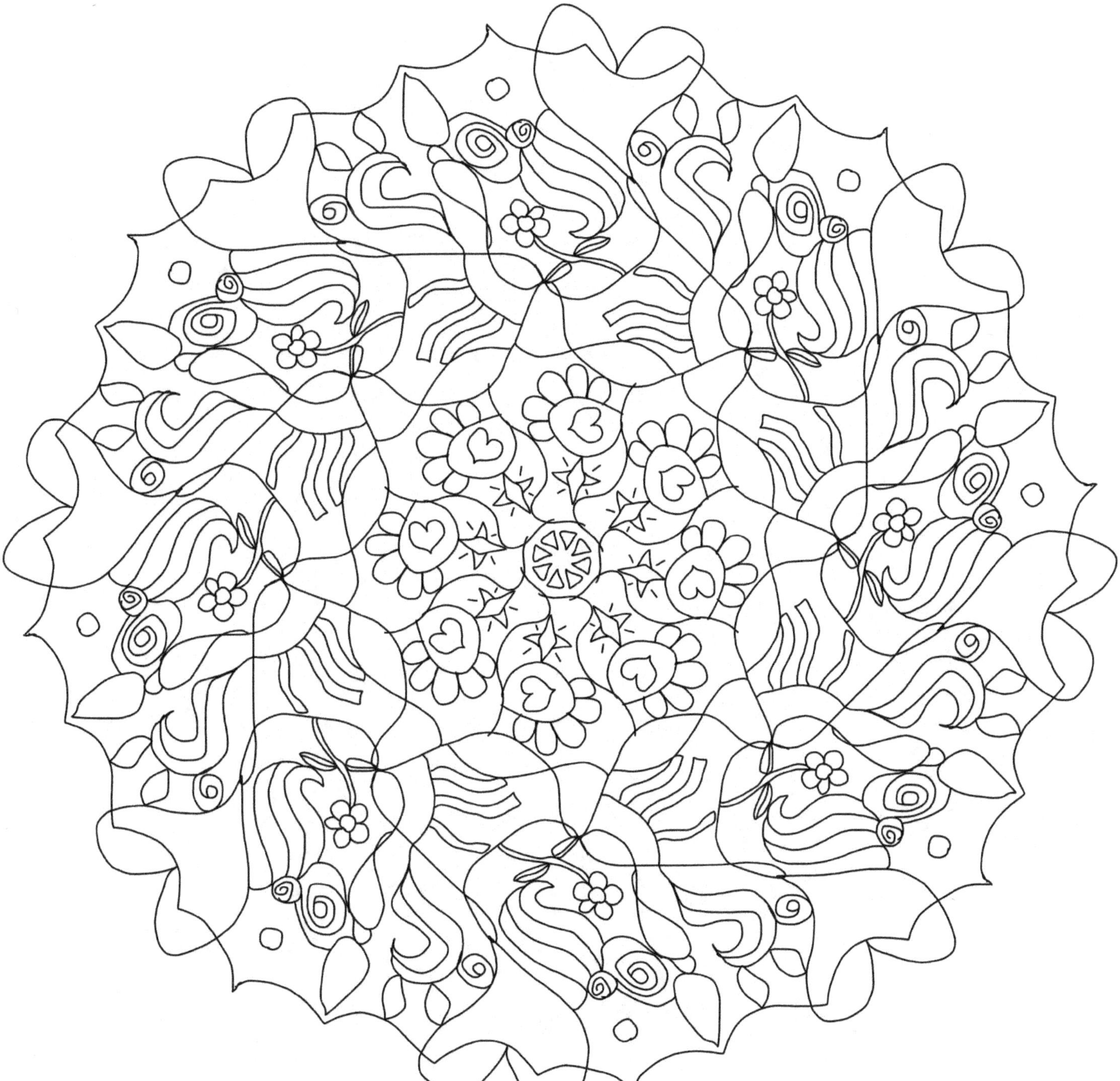

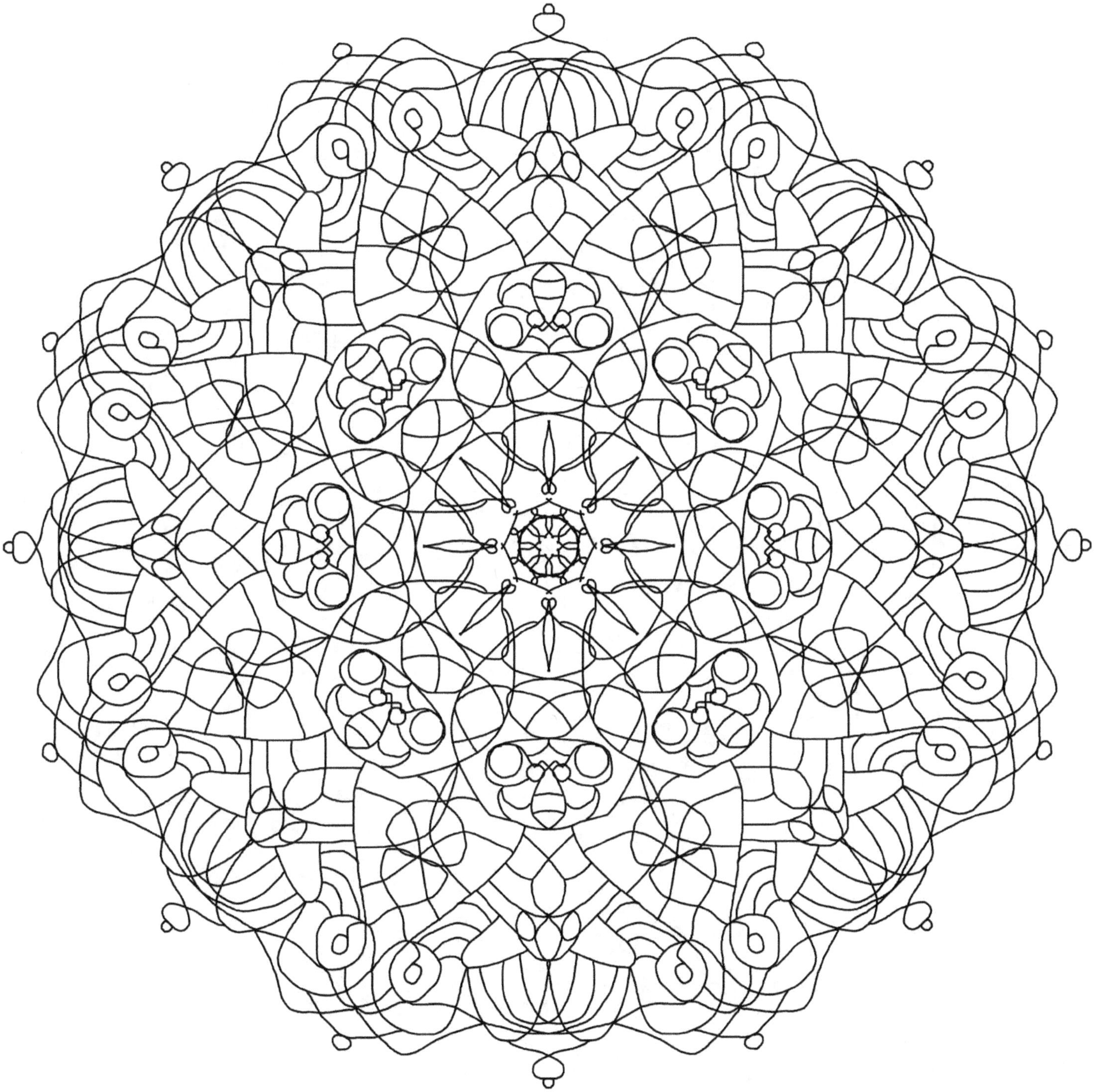

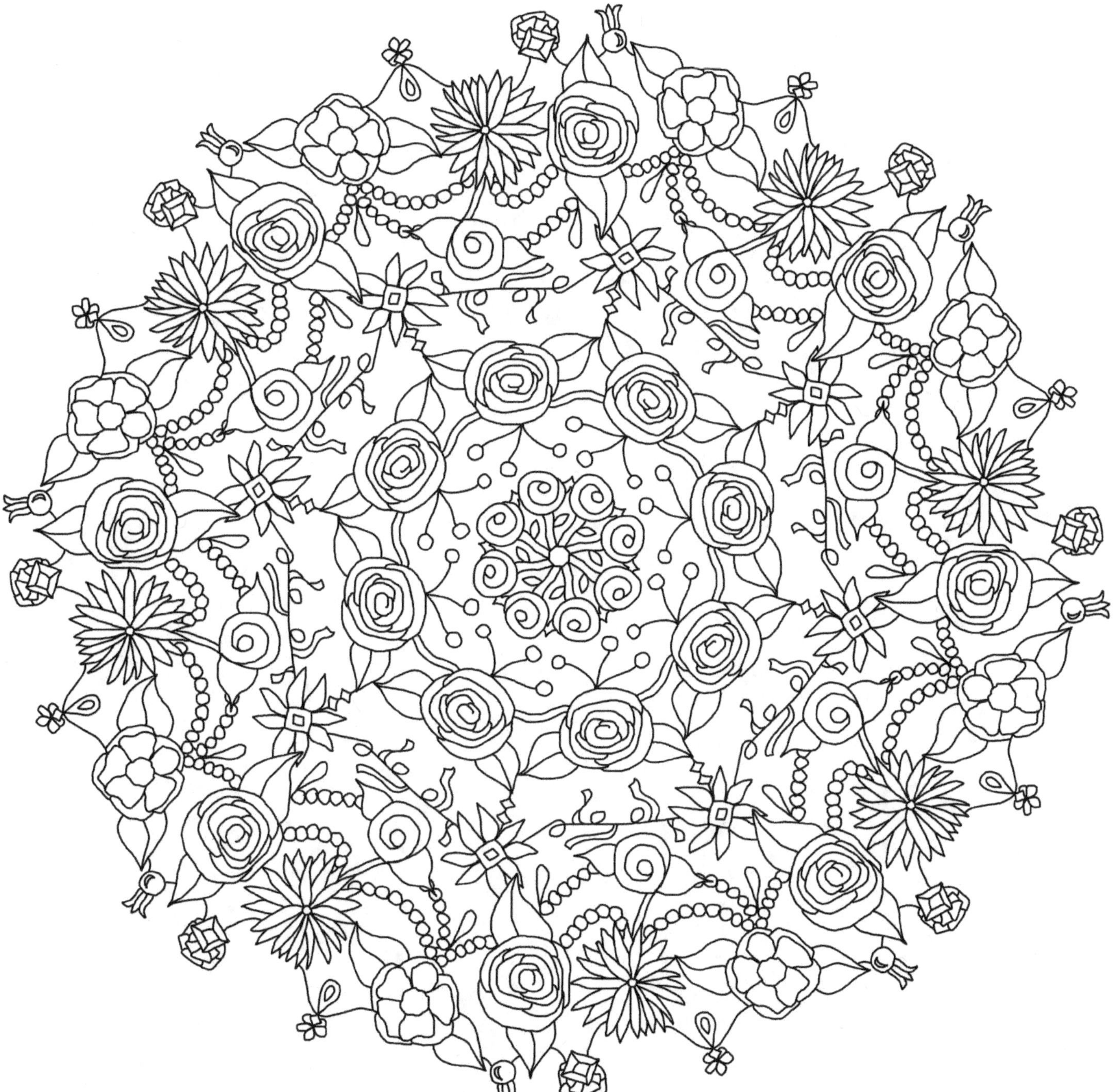

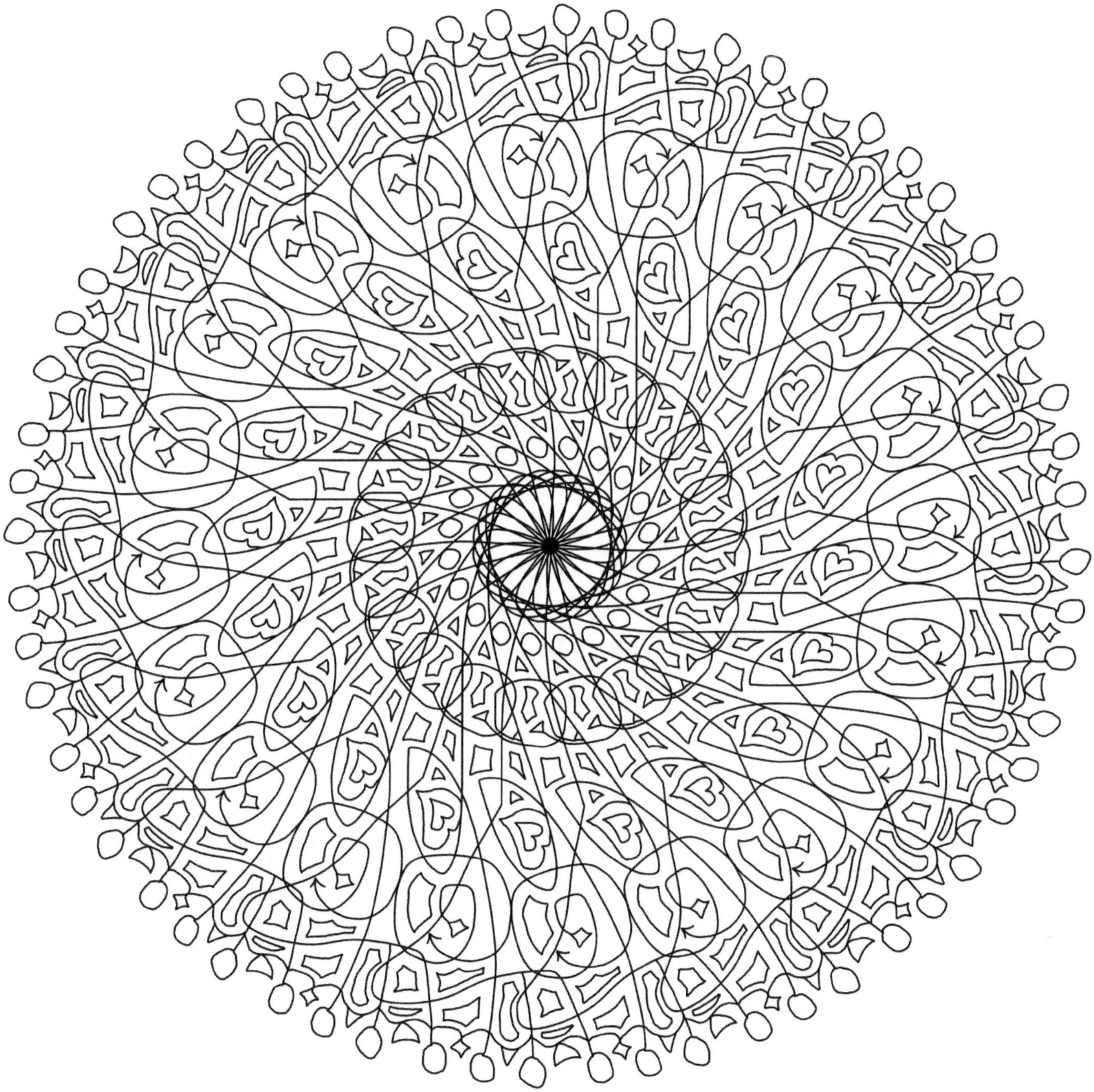

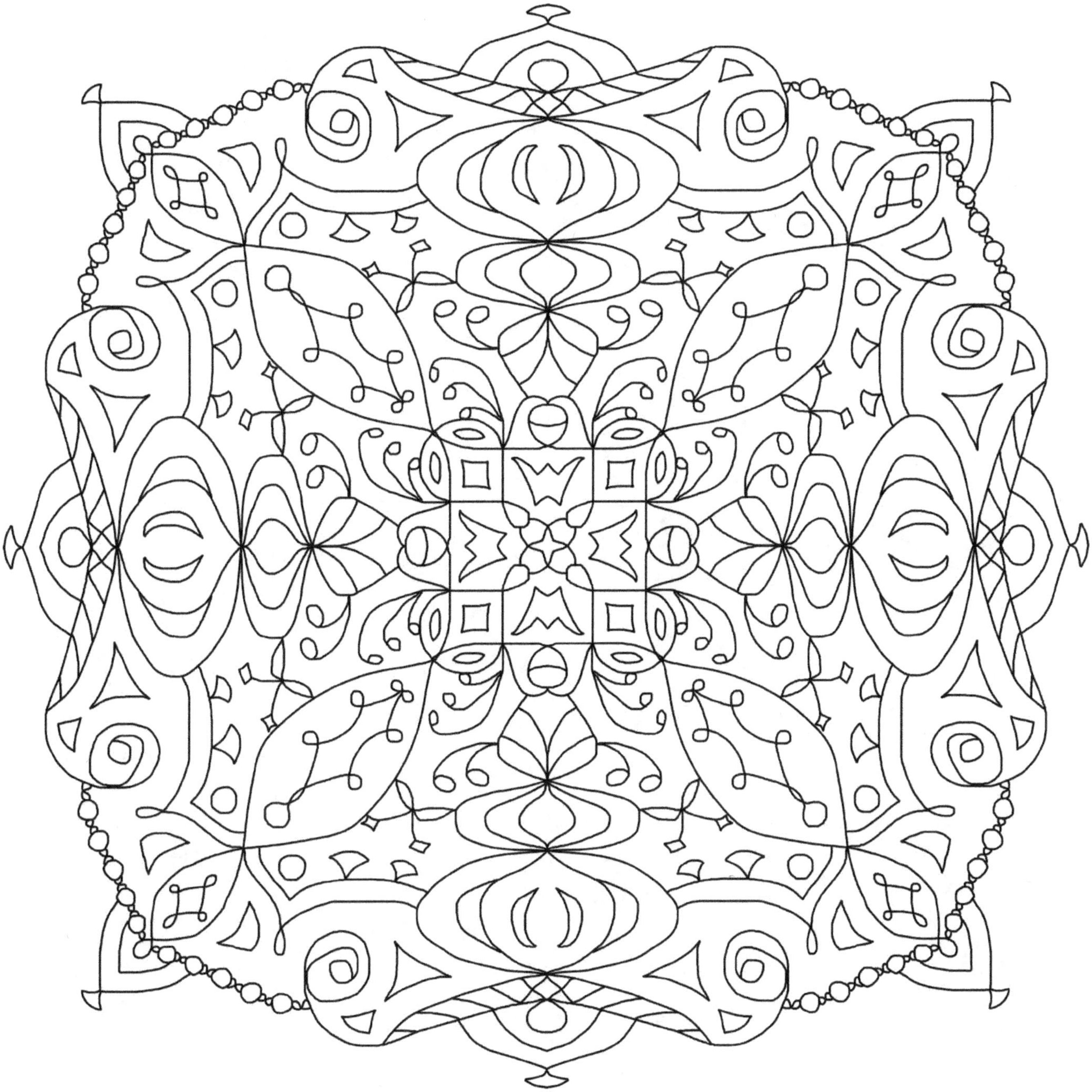

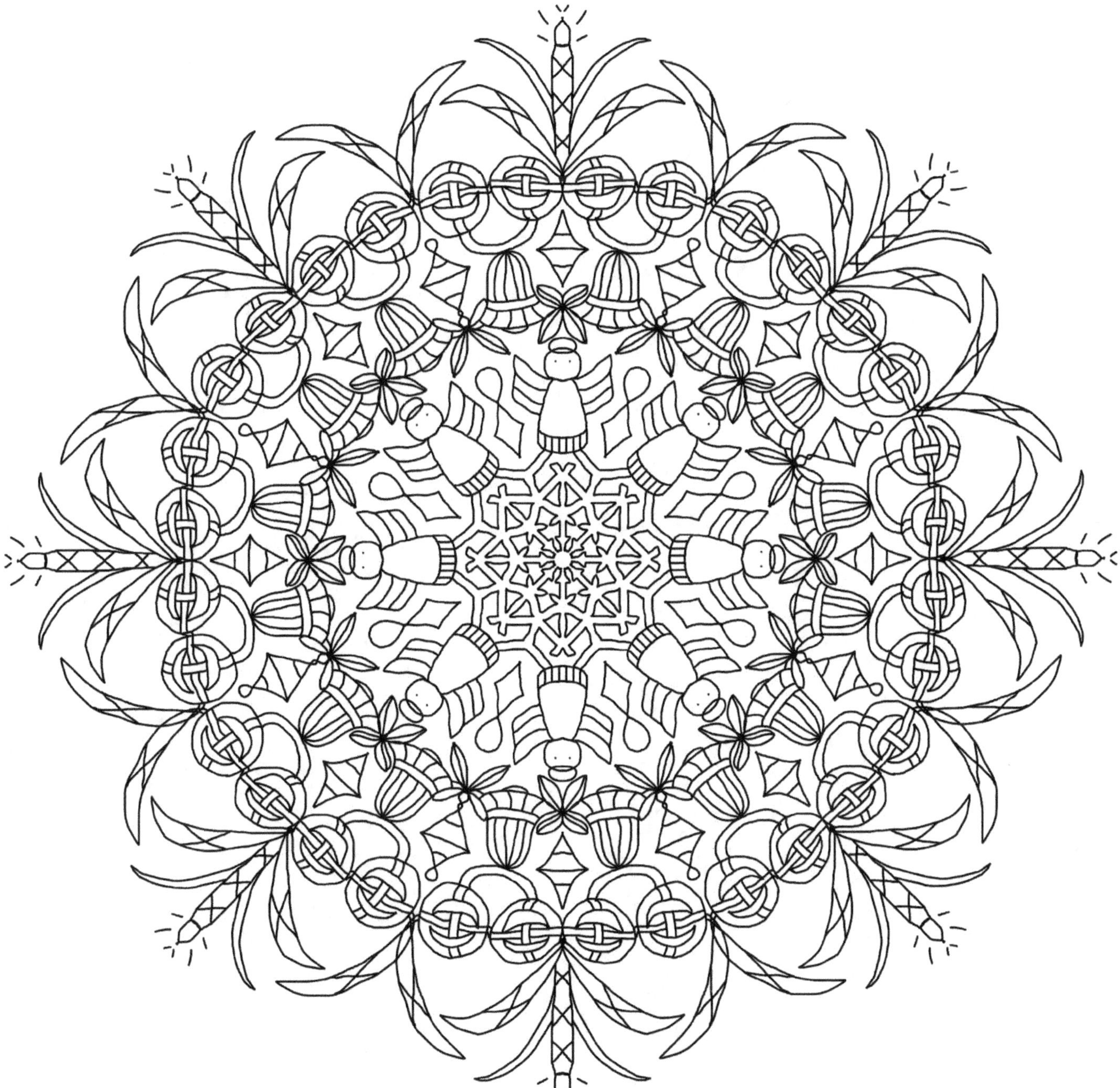

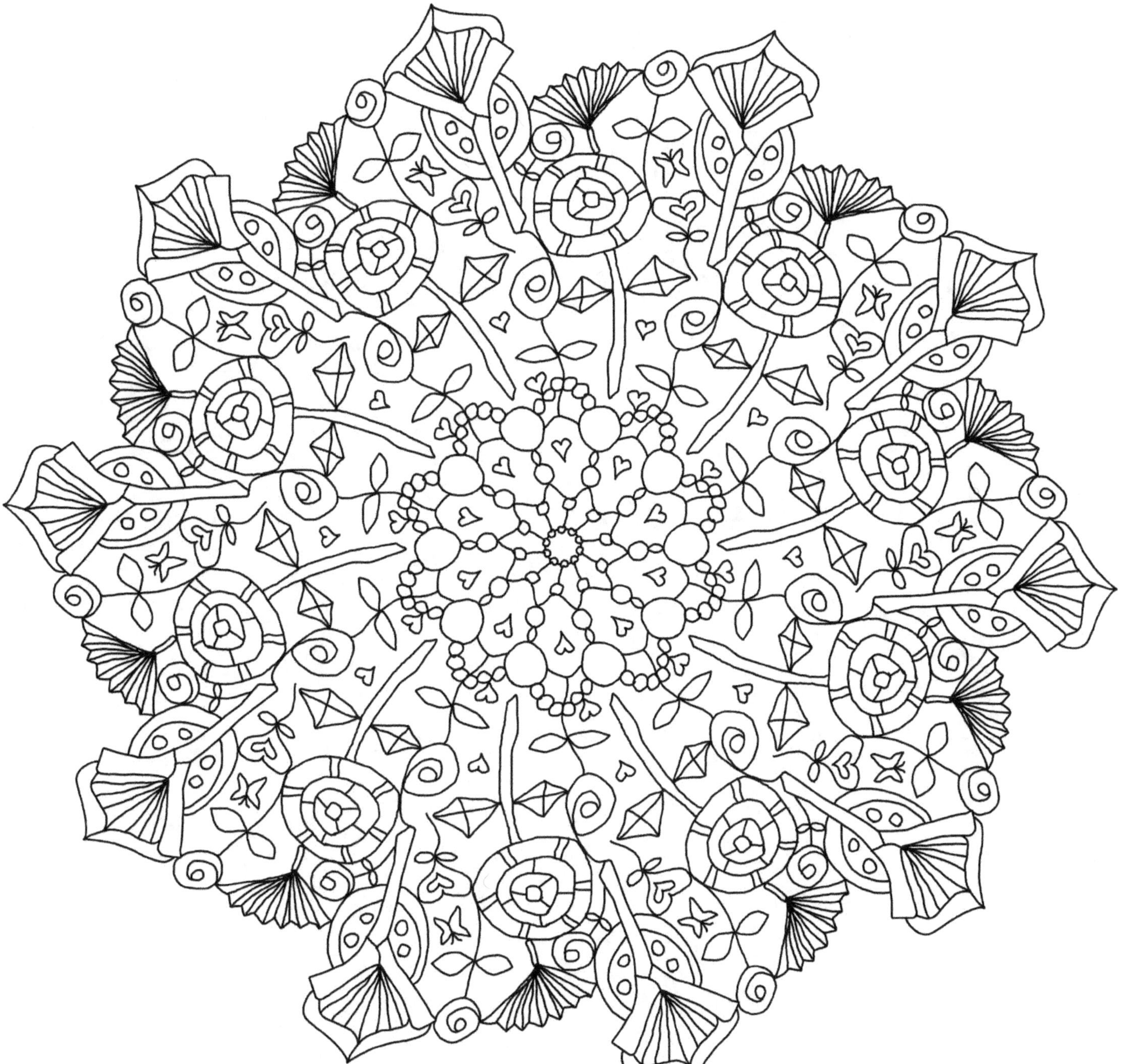

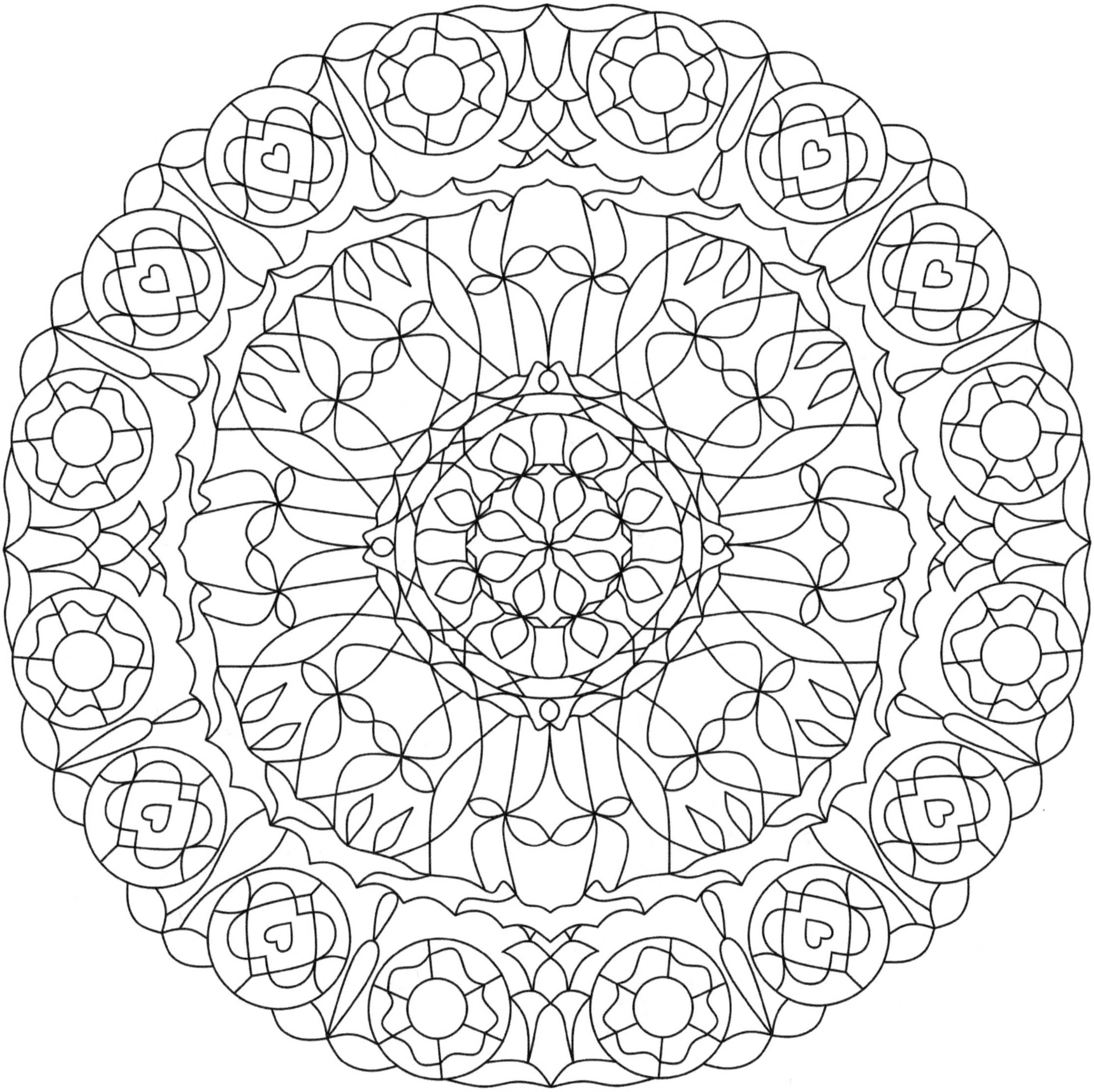

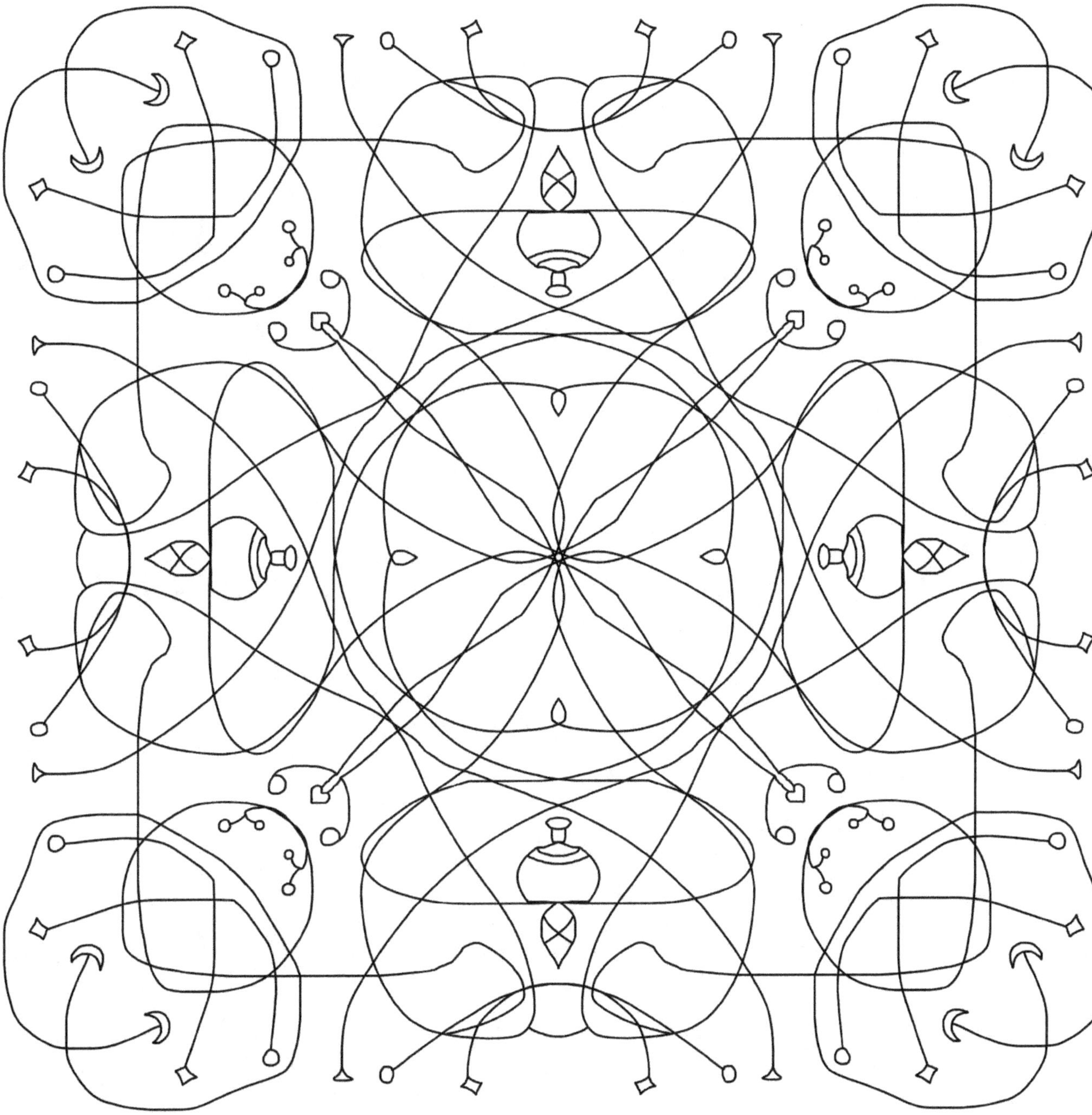

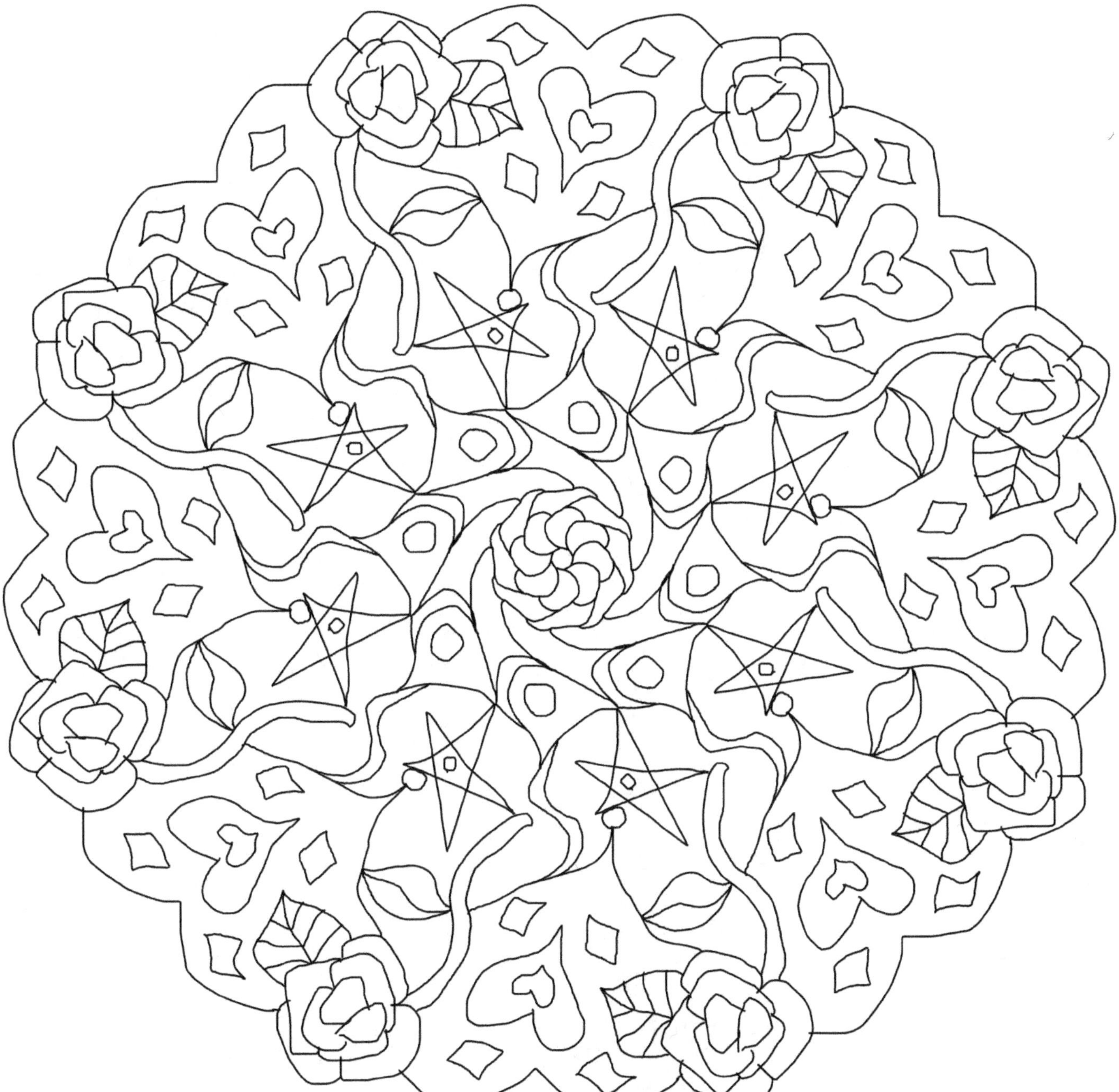

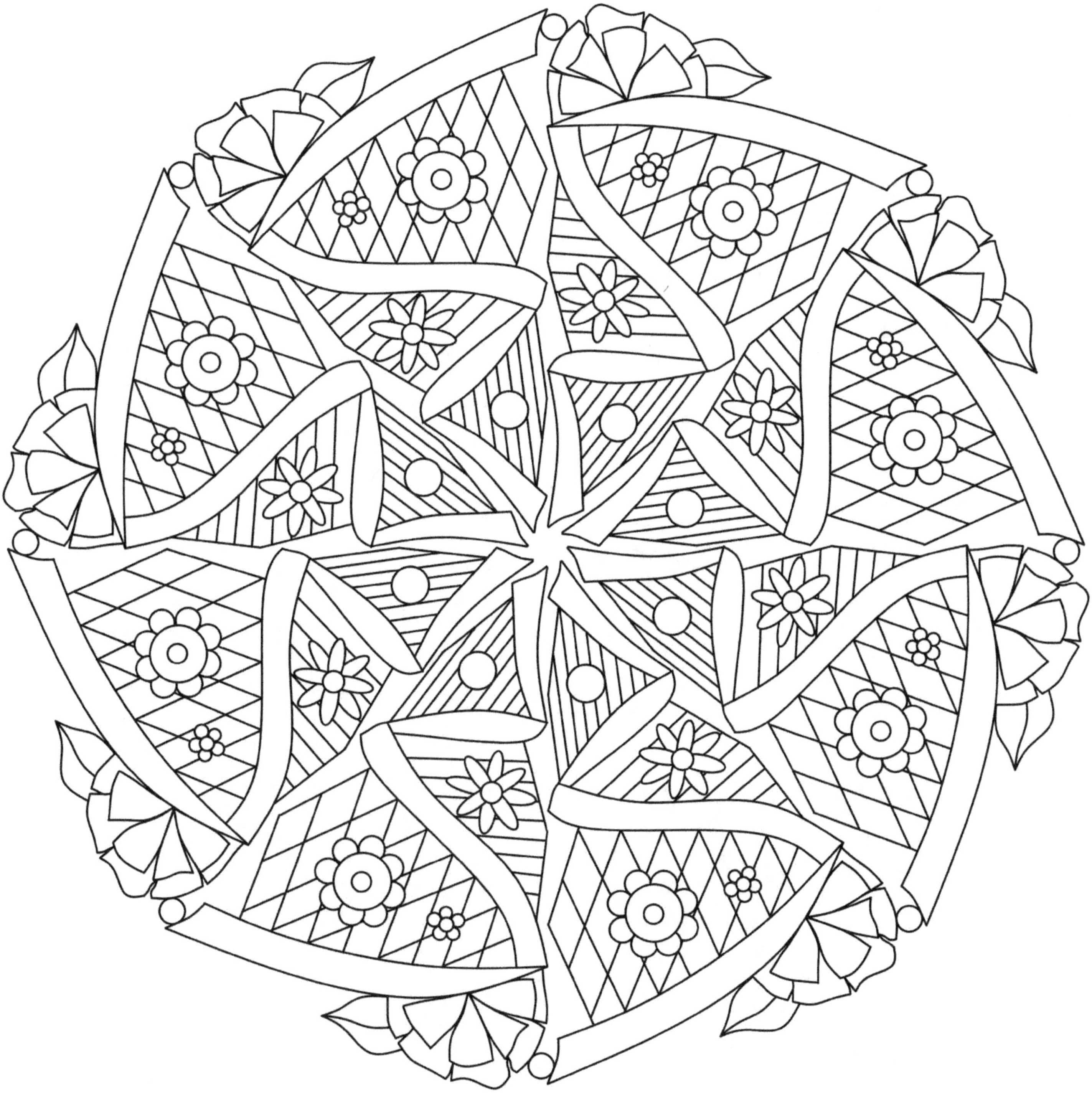

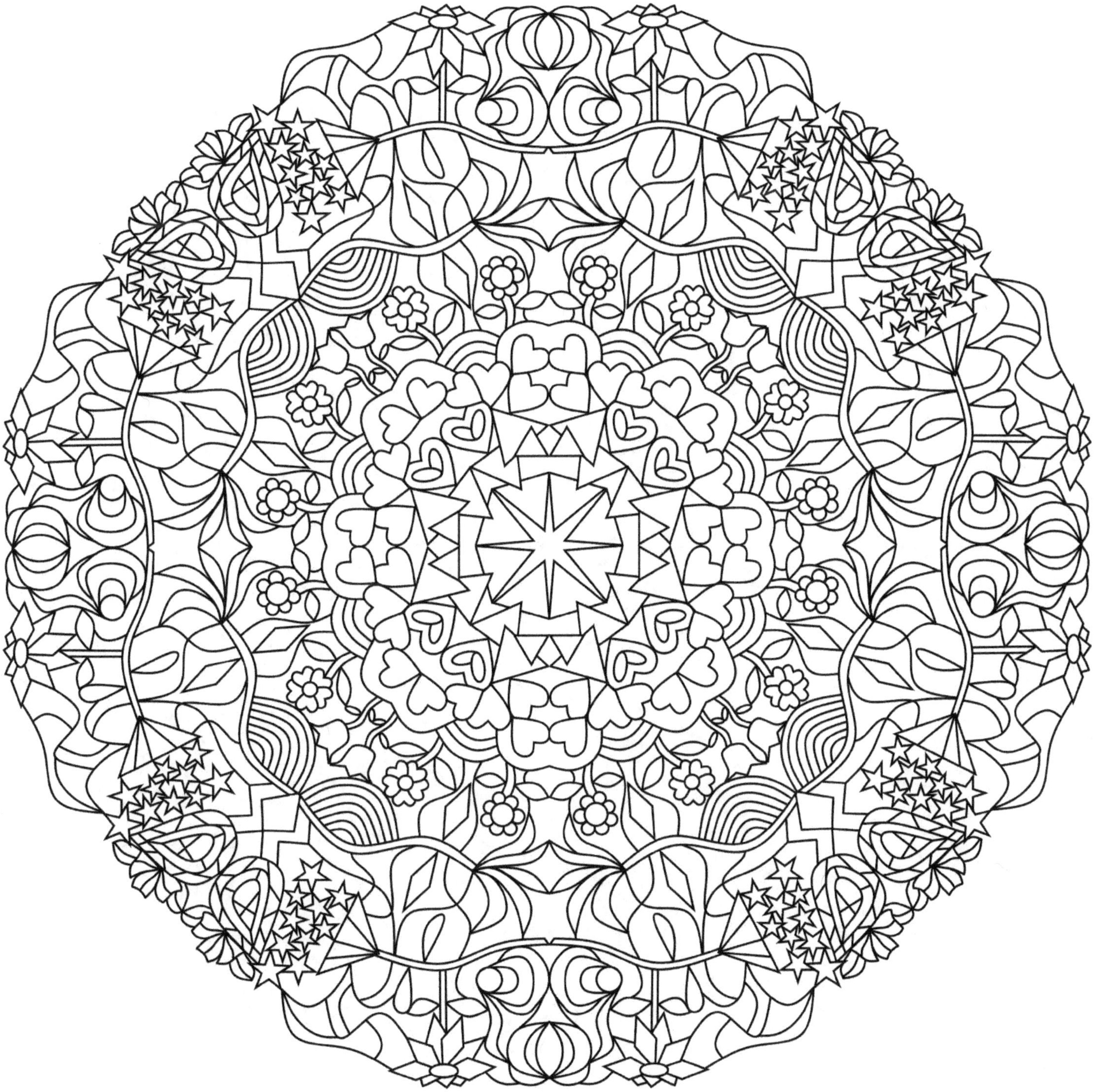

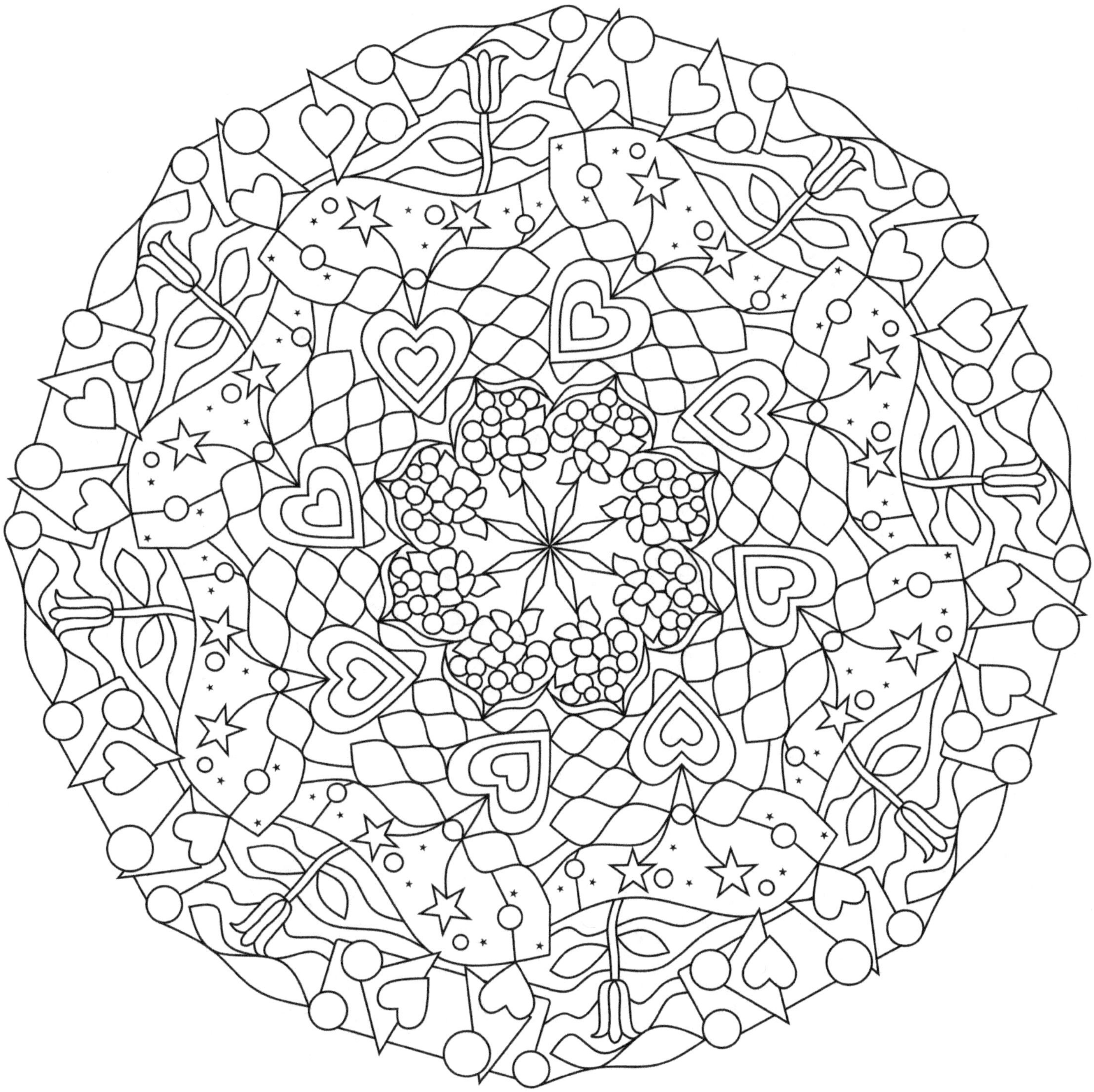

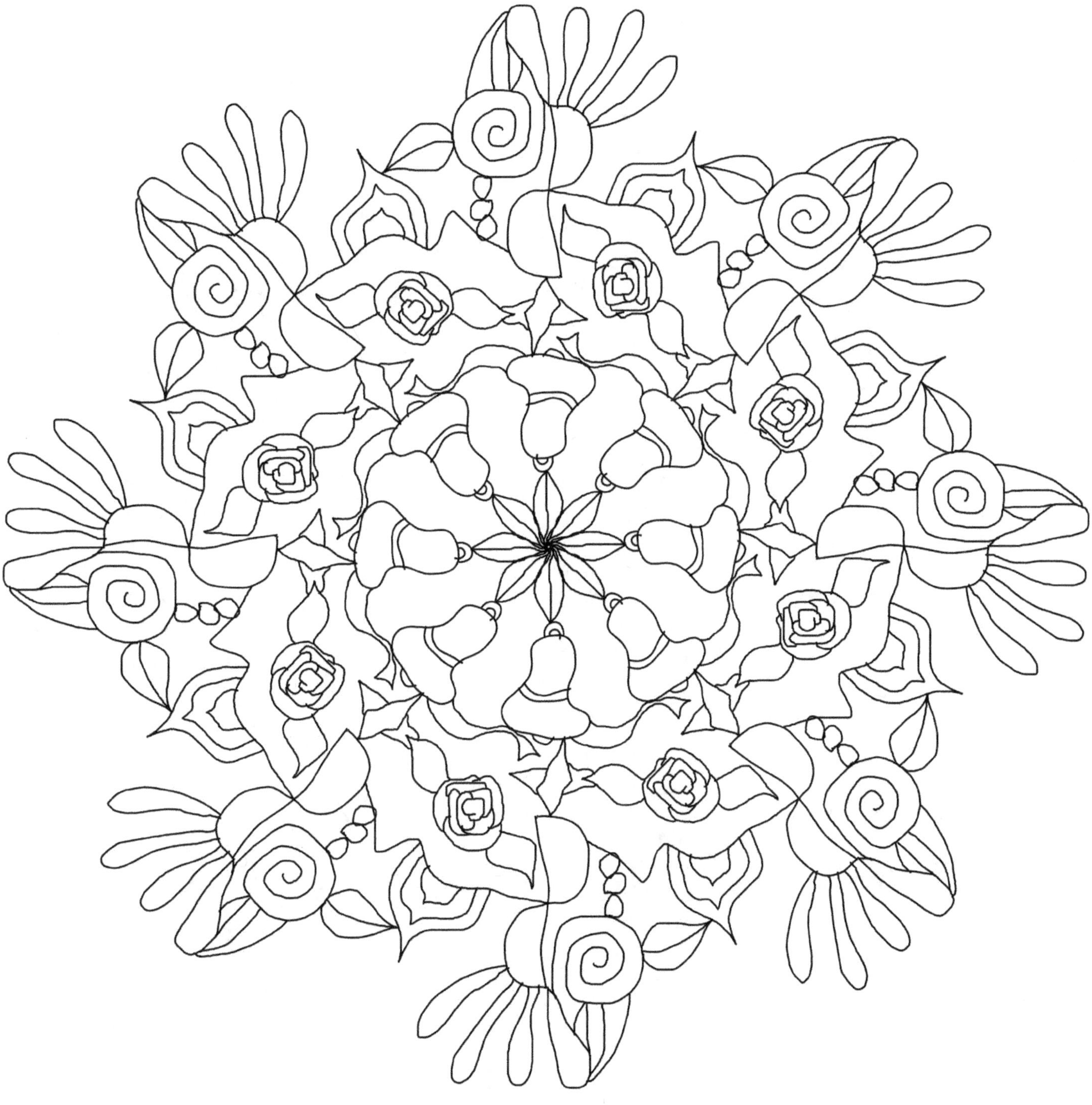

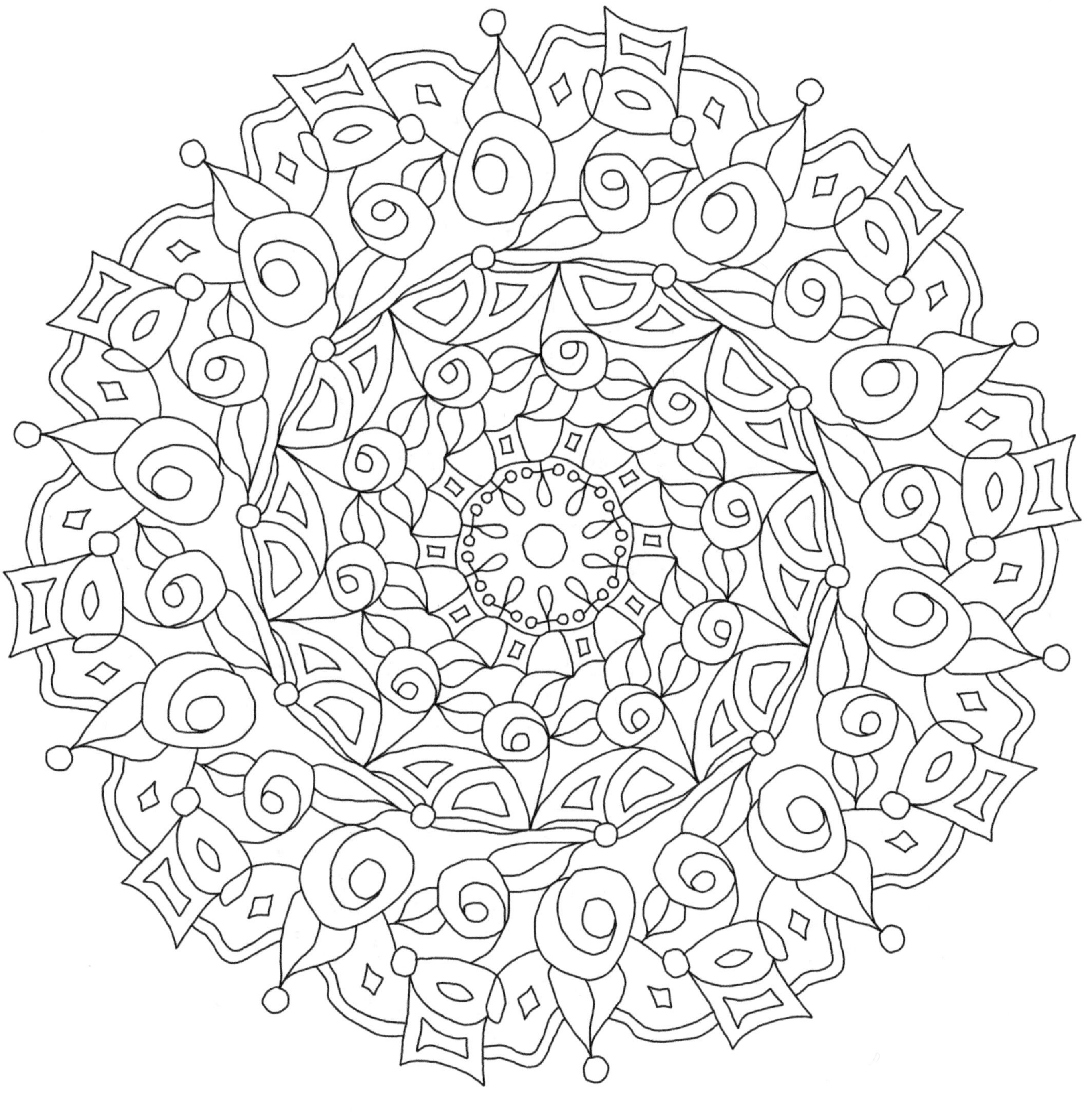

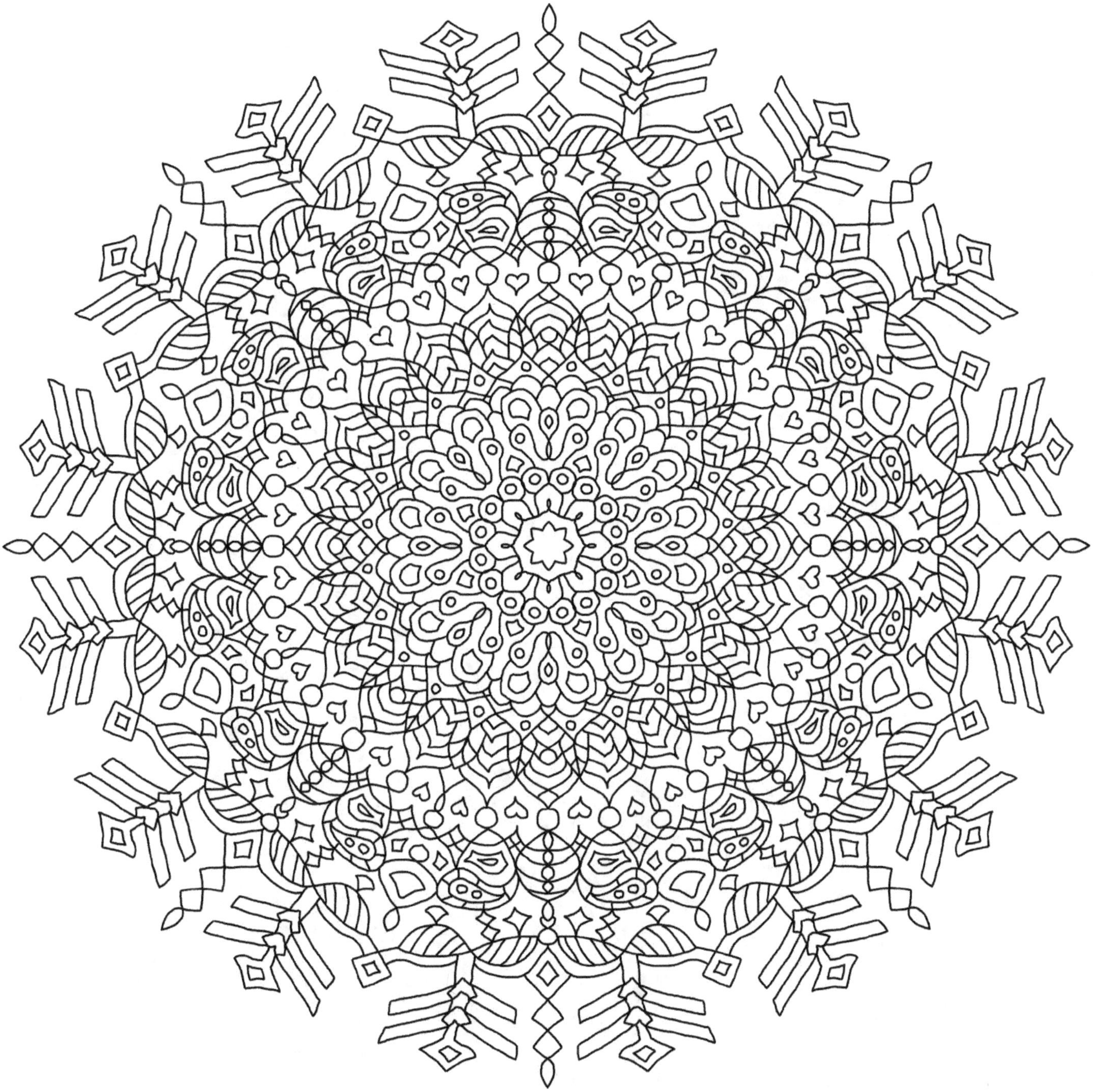

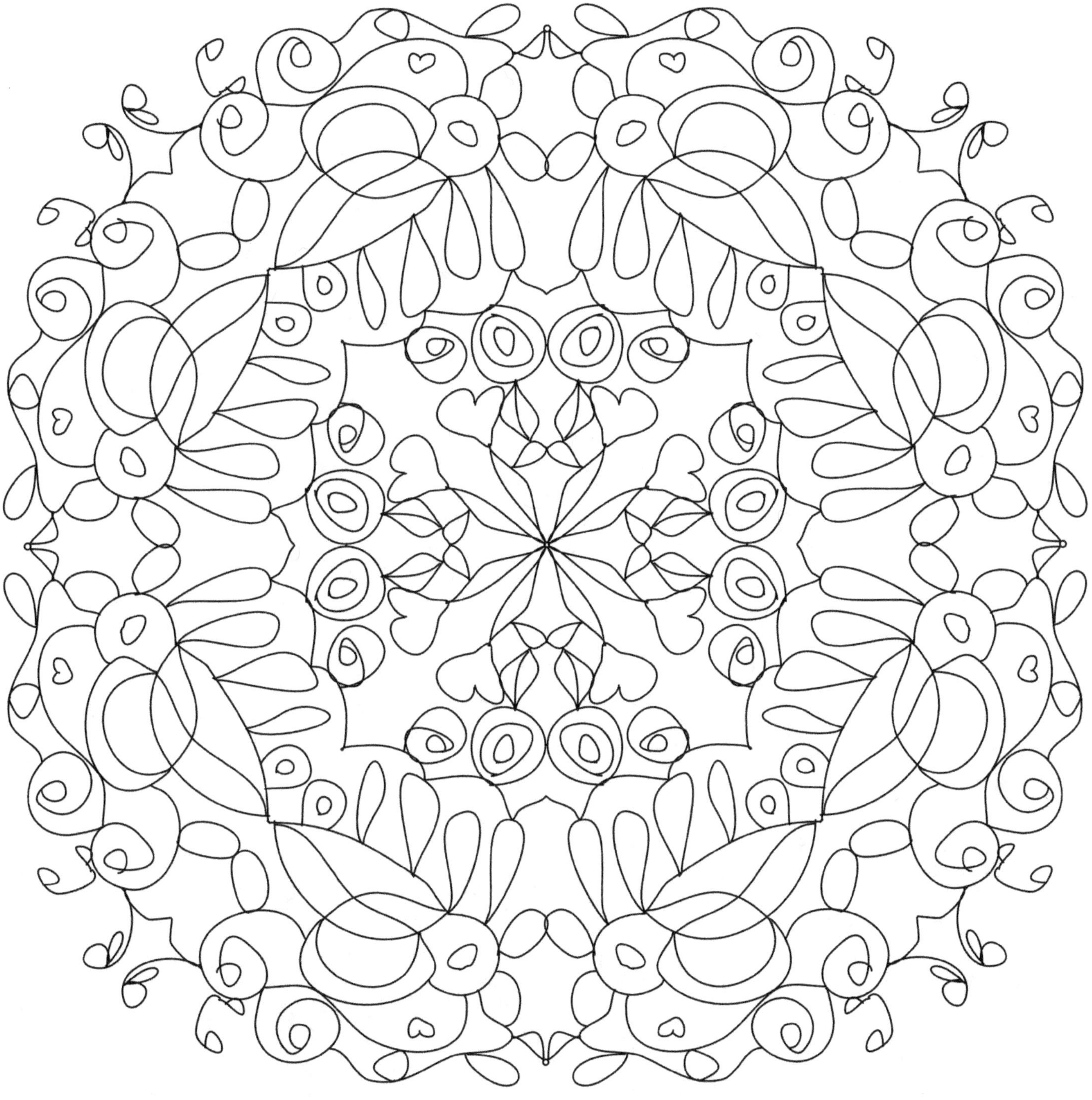

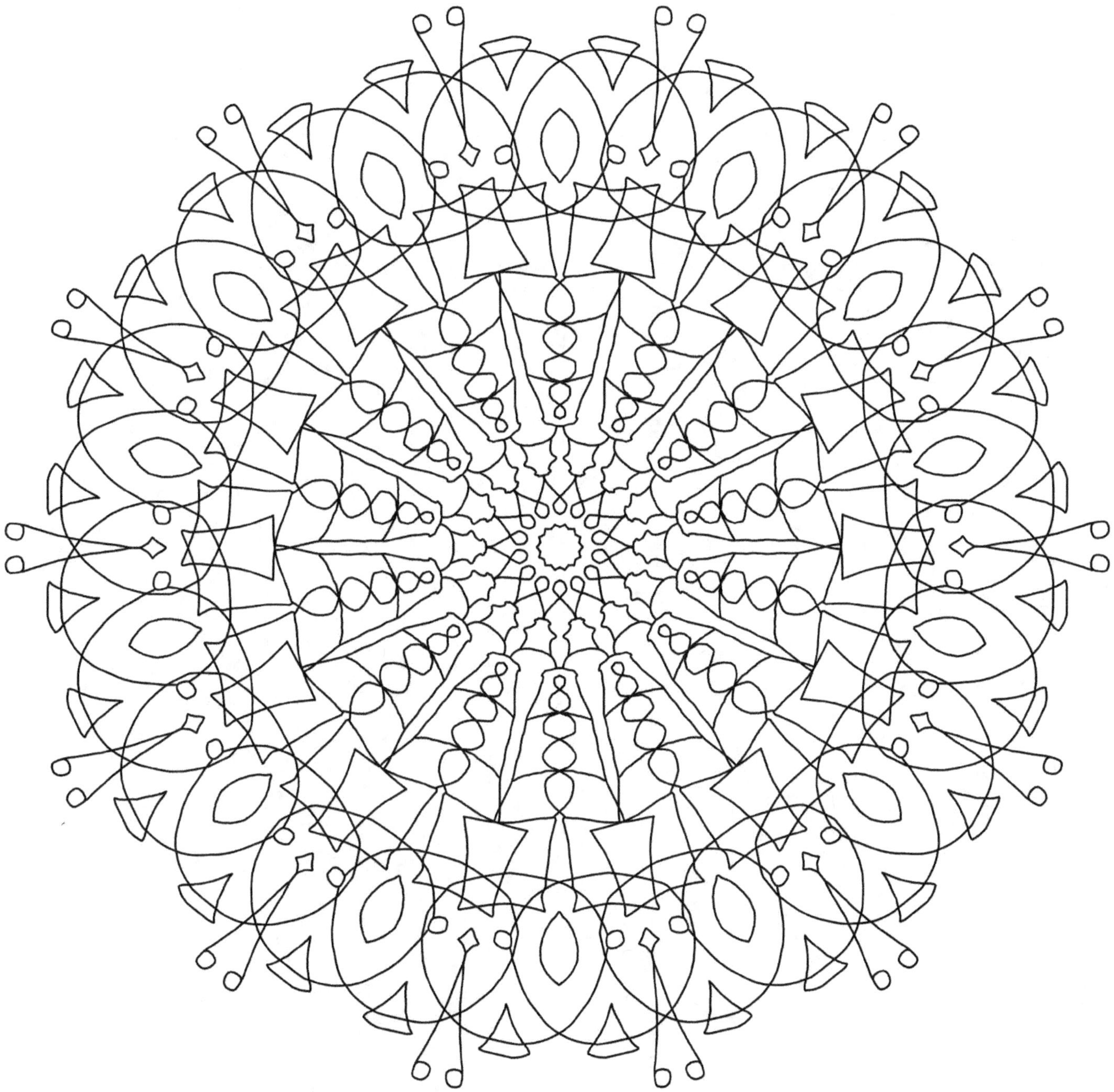

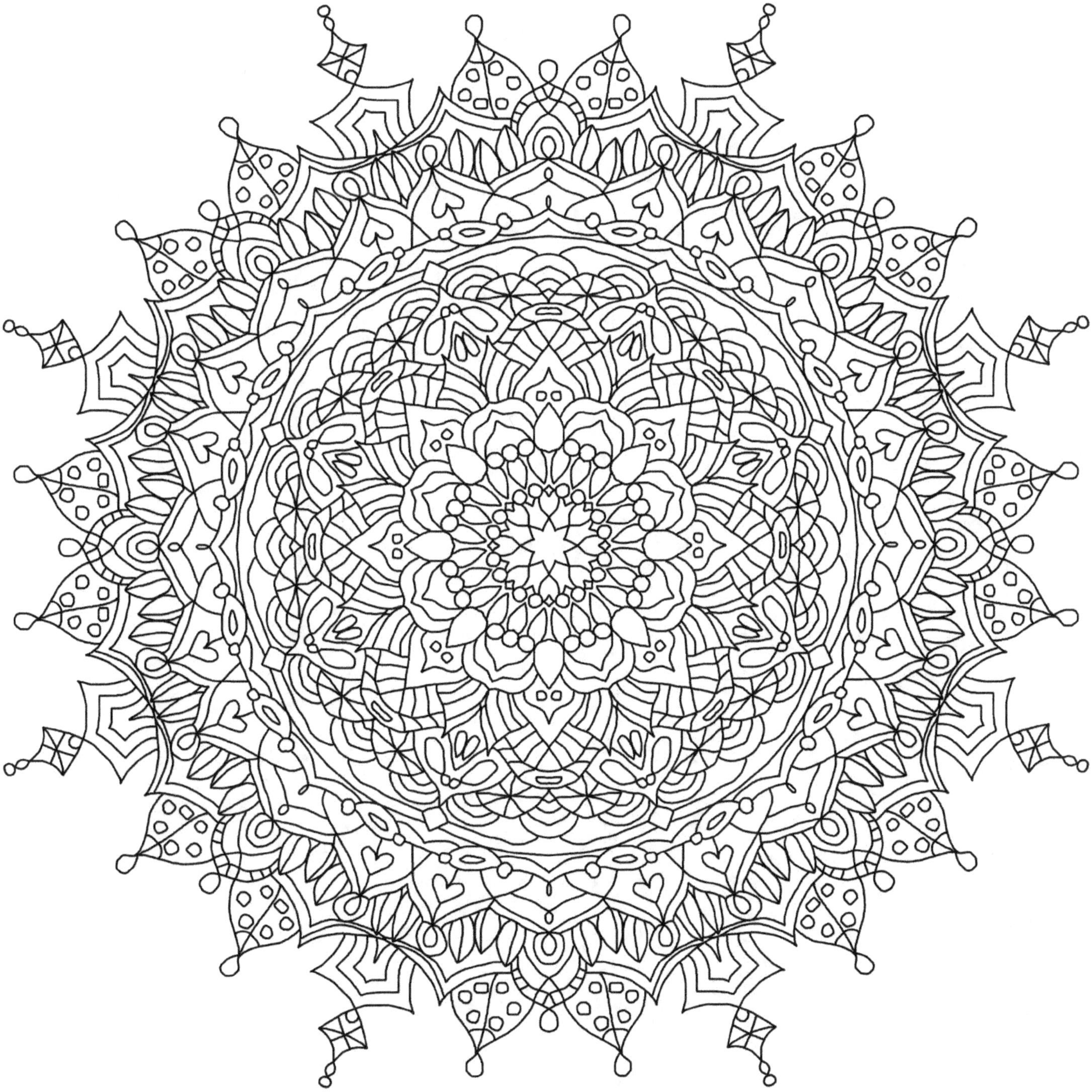

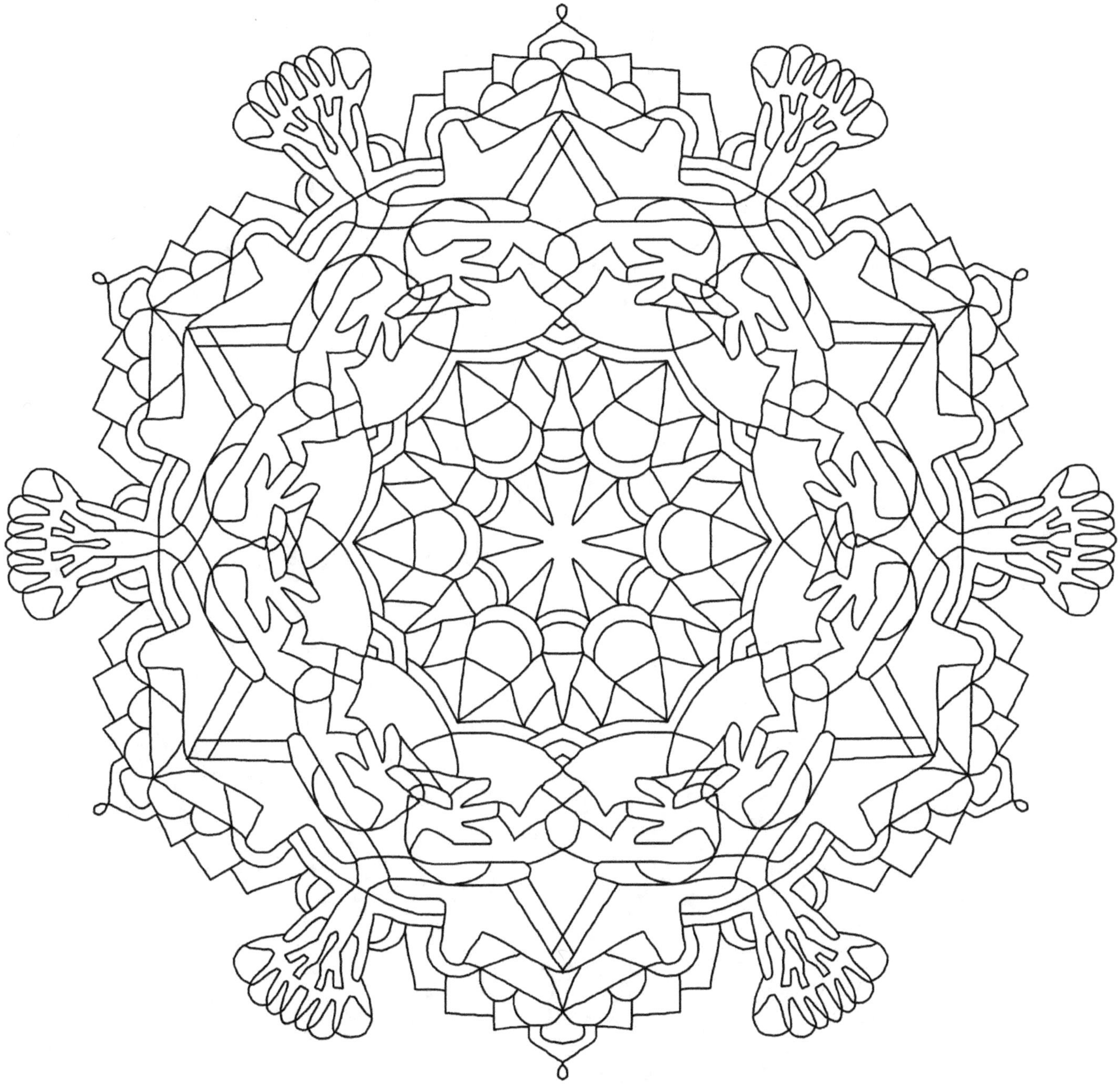

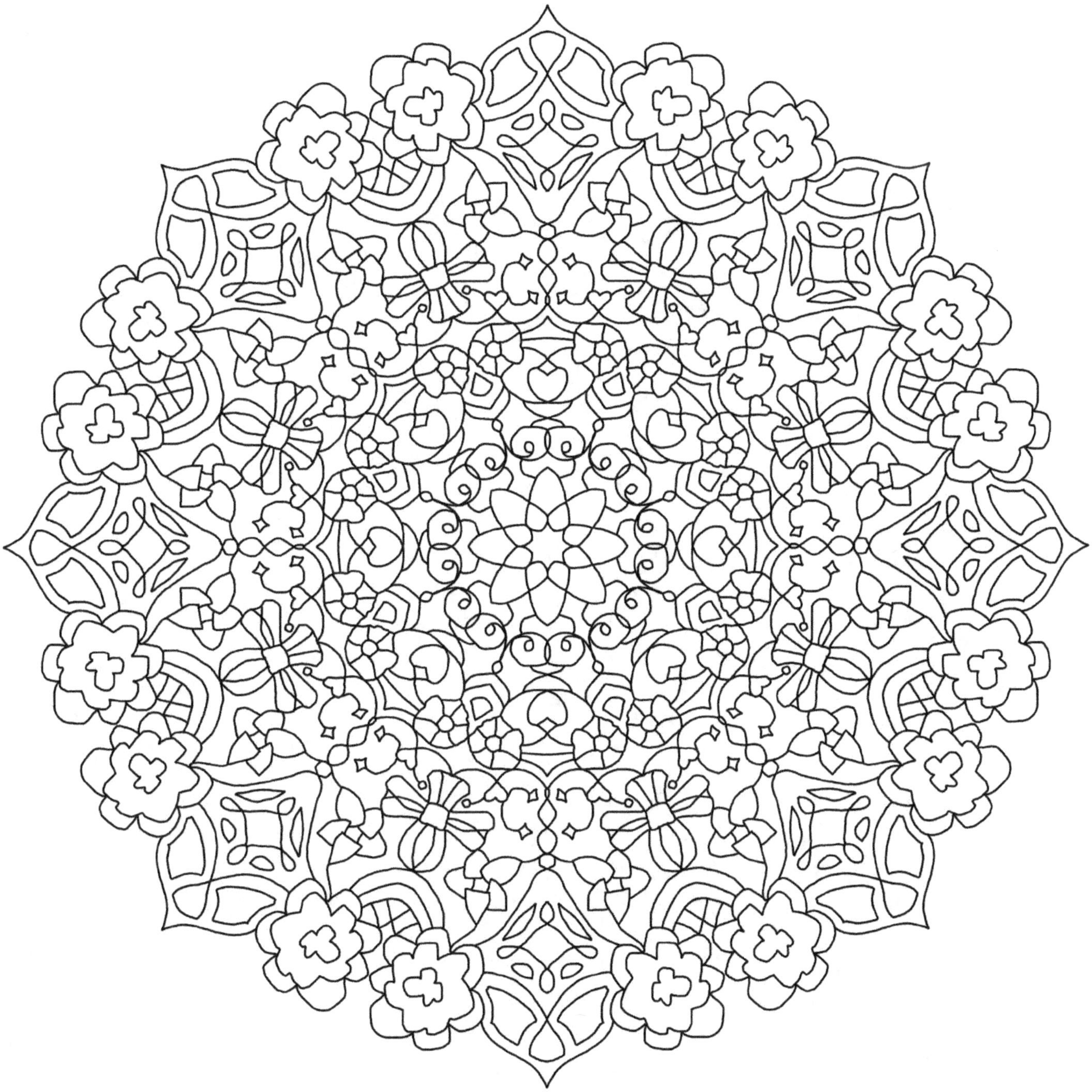

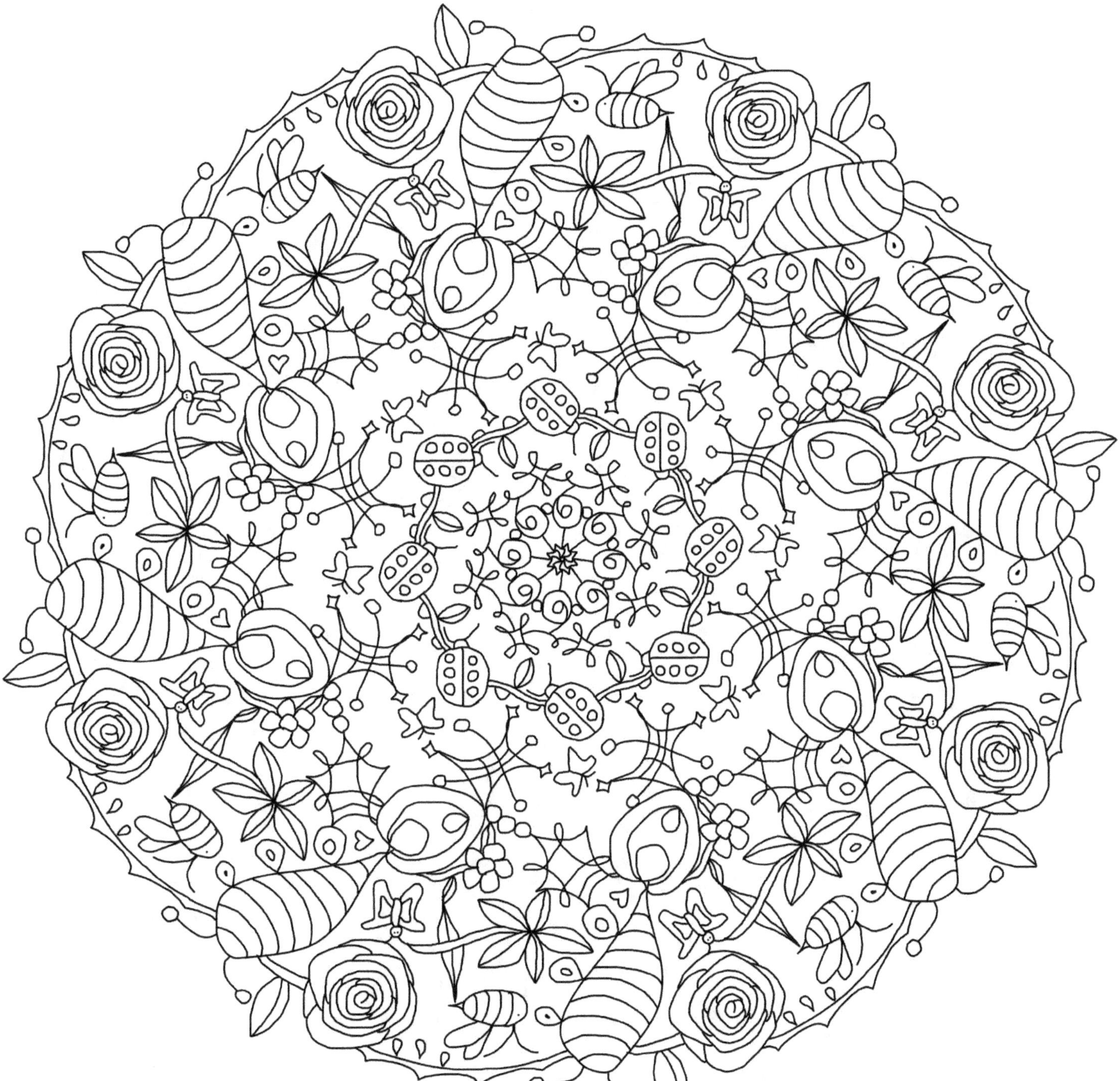

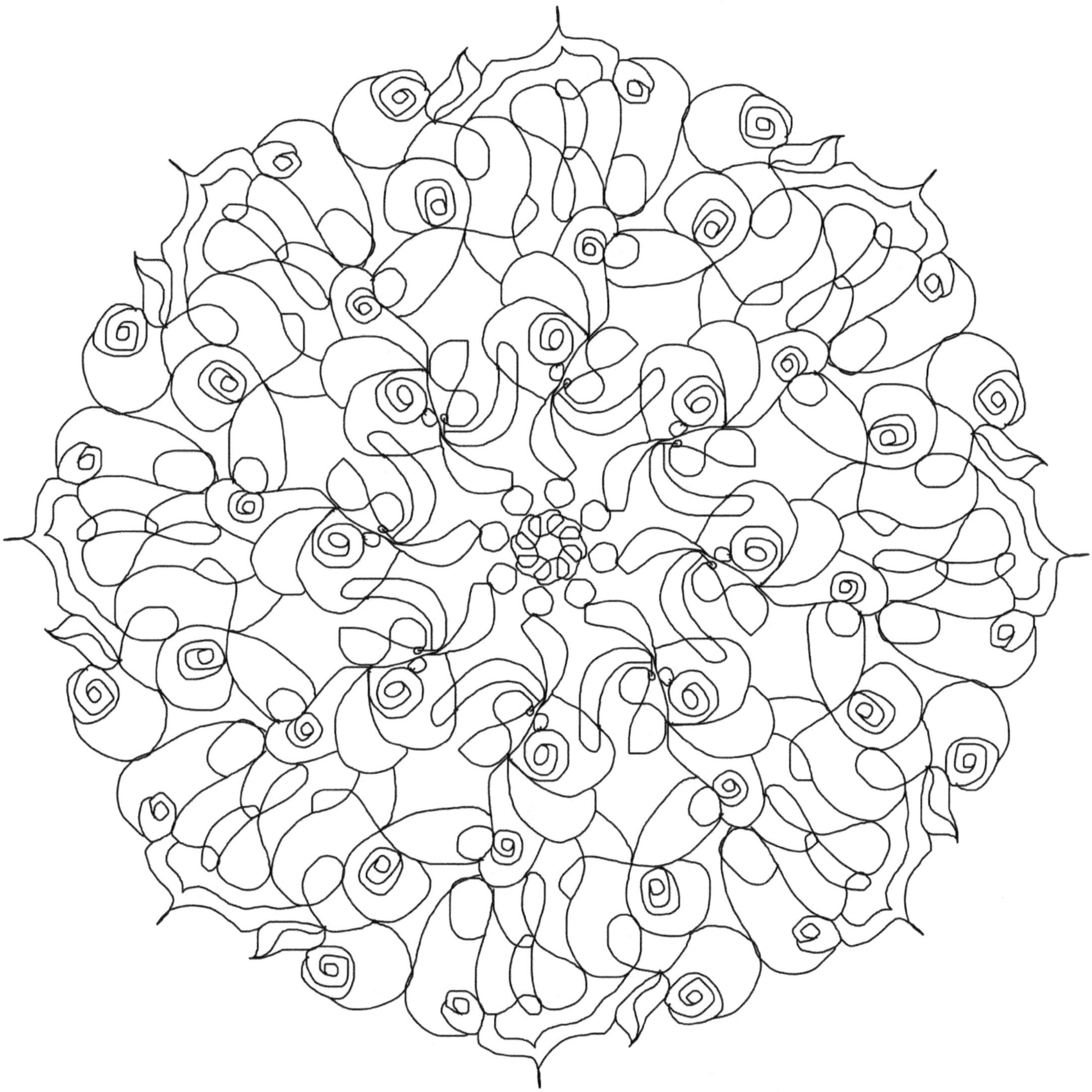

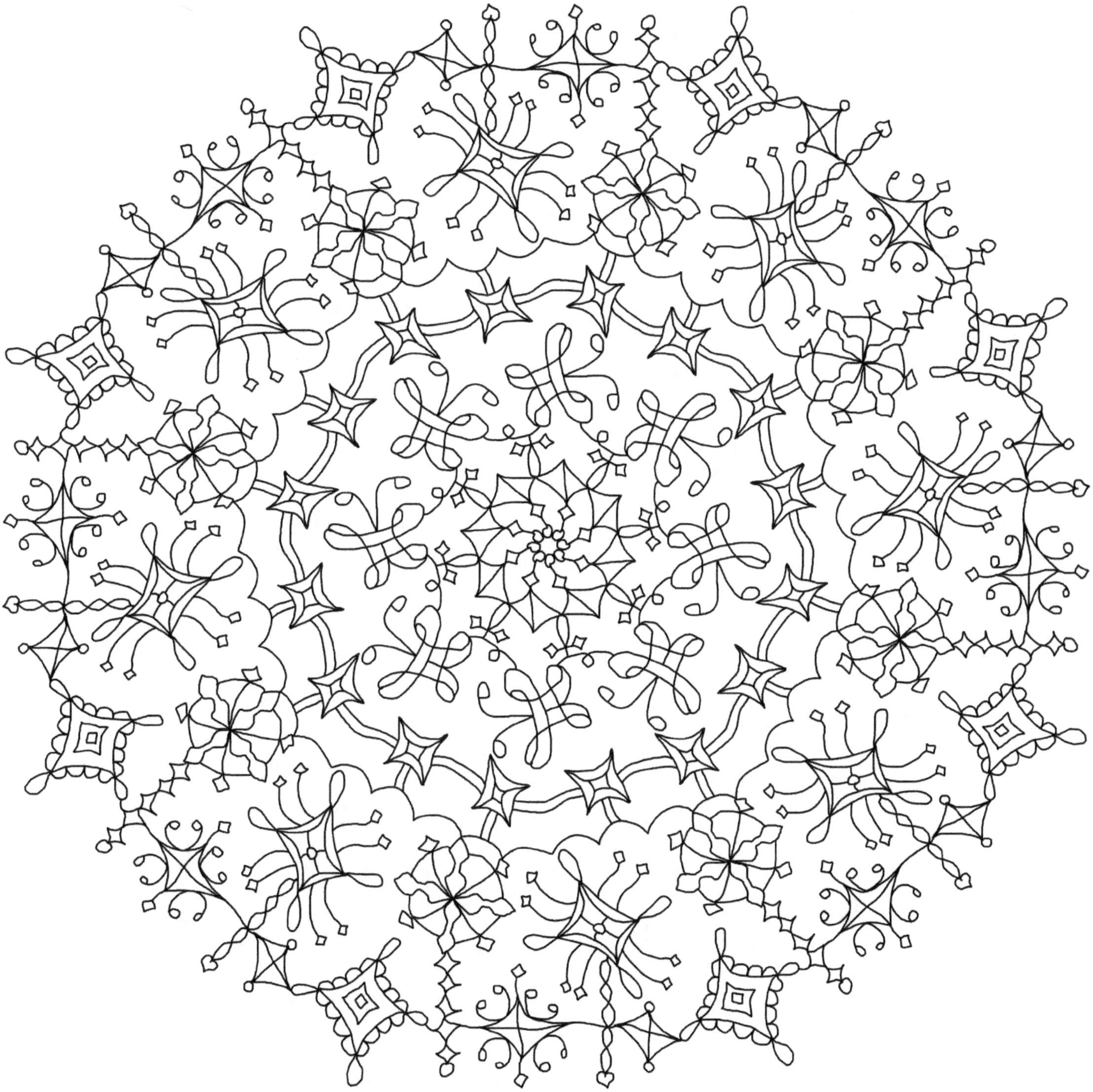

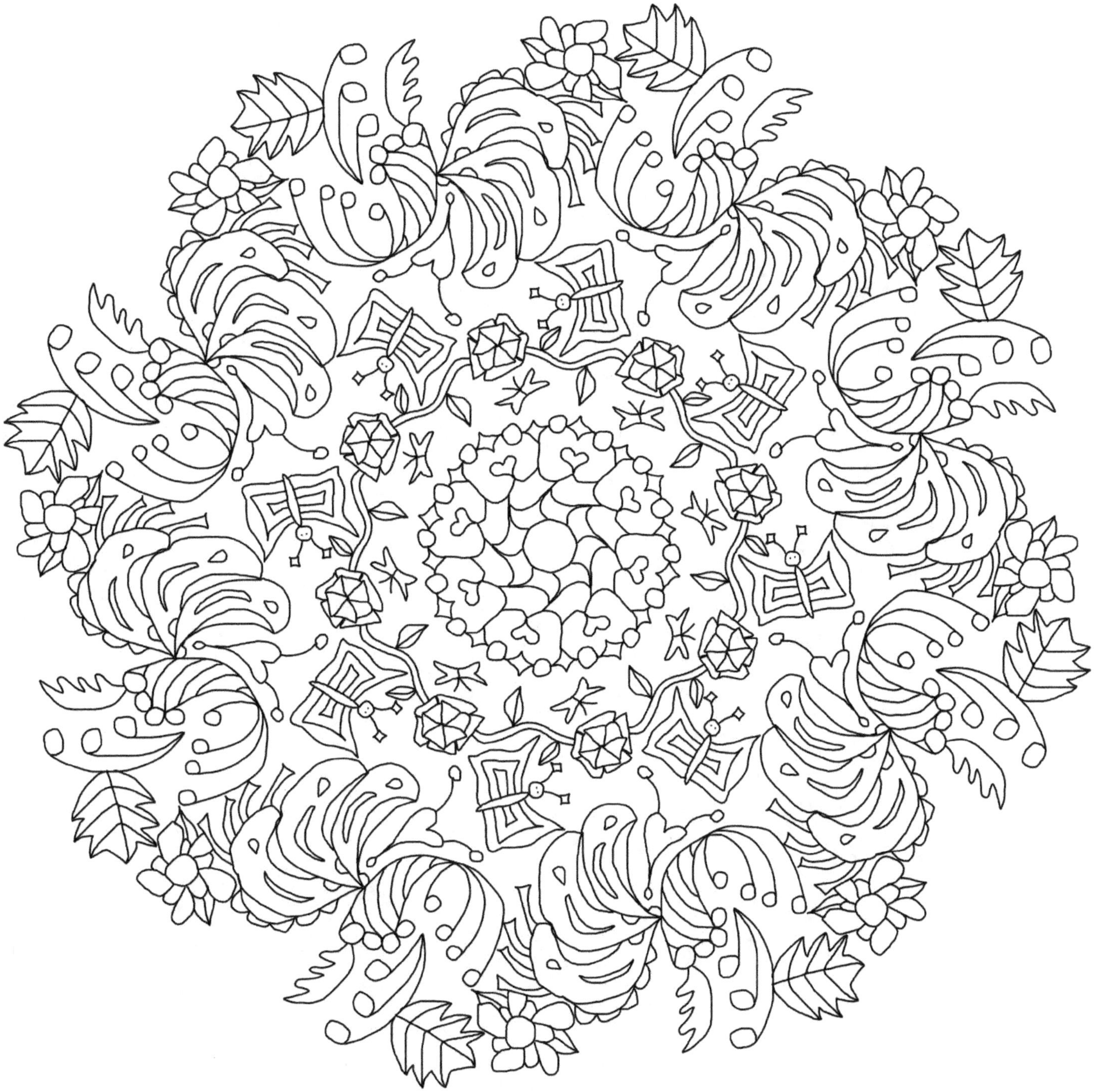

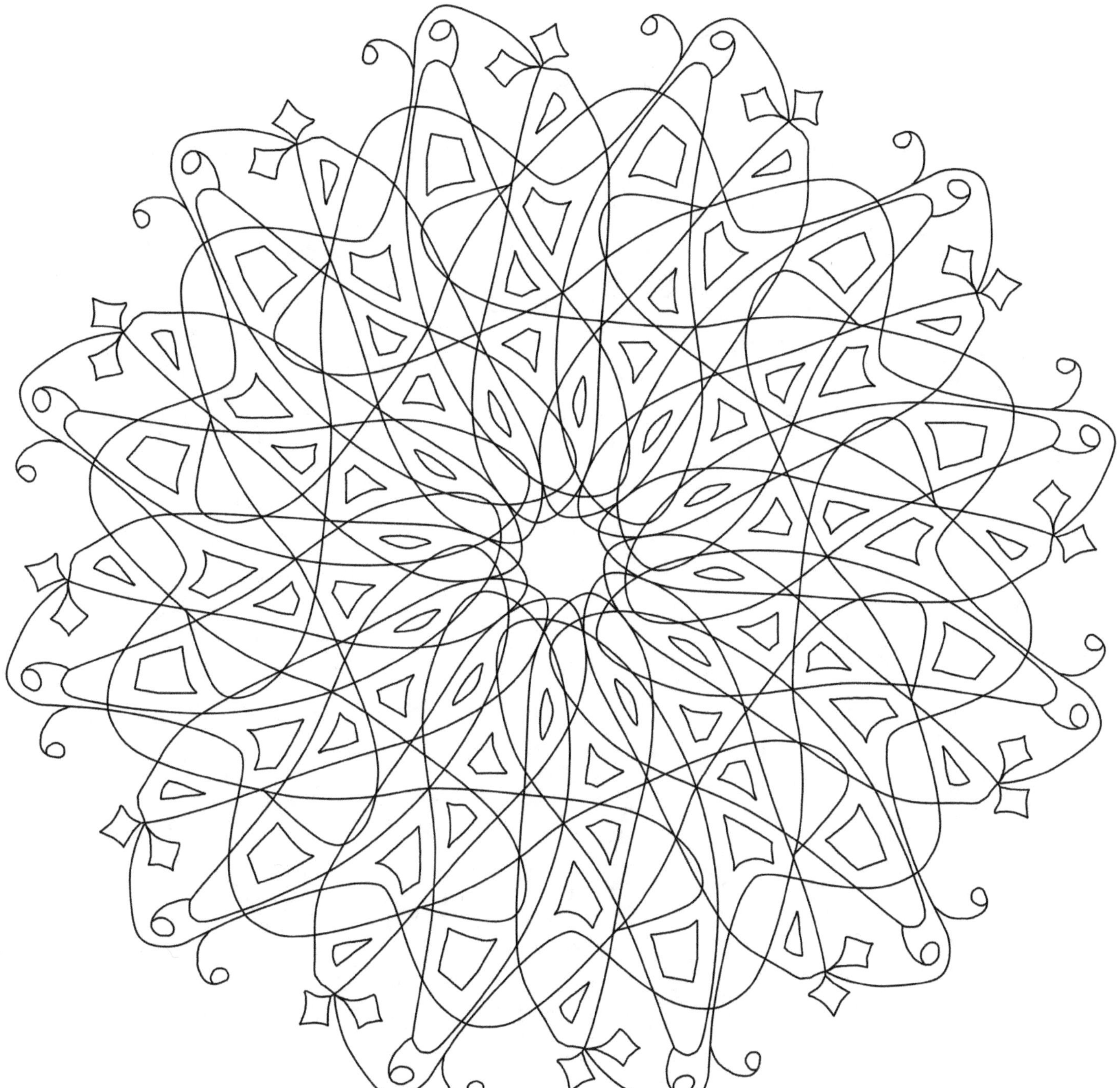

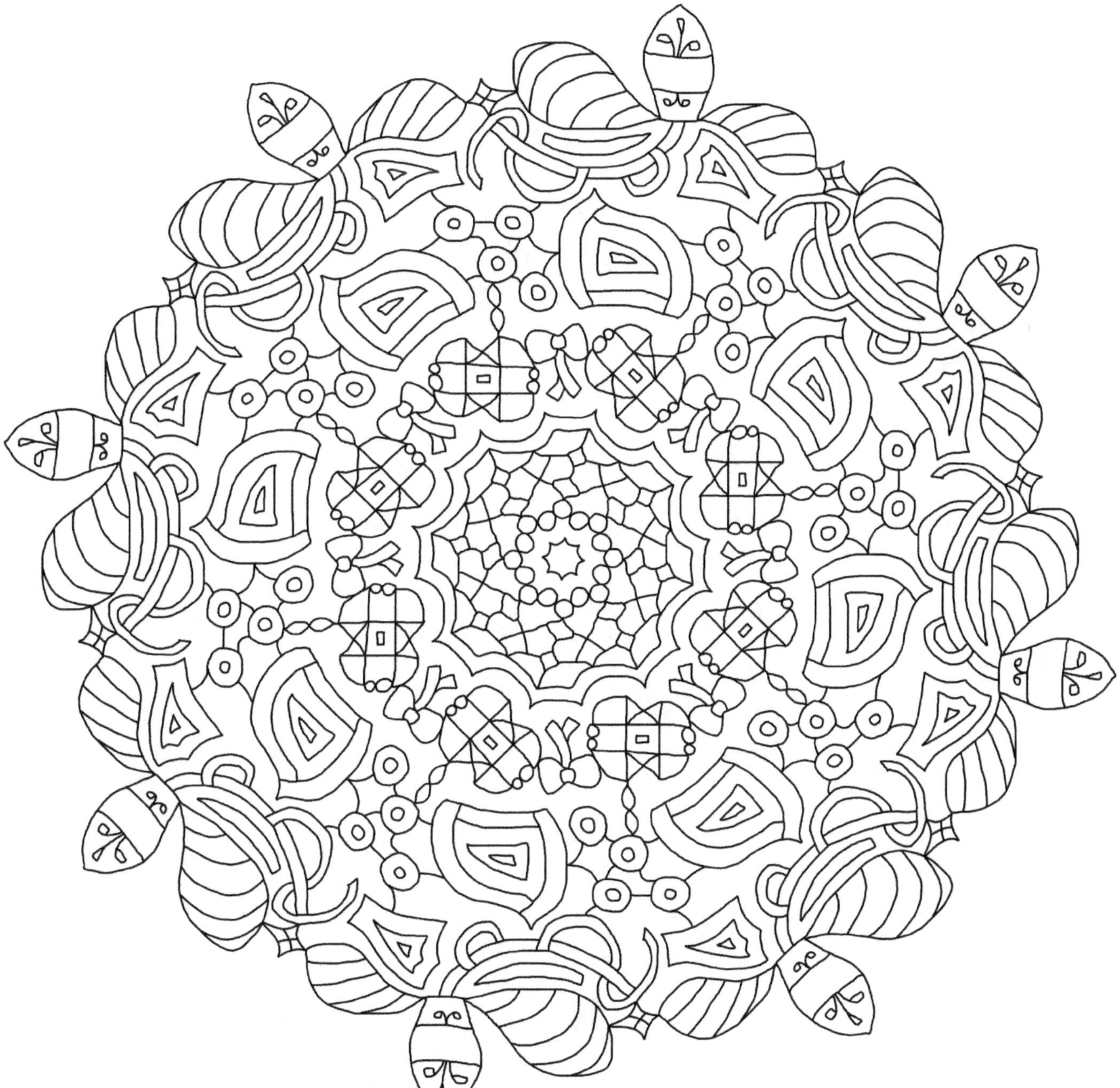

www.ingramcontent.com/pod-product-compliance
Lightning Source LLC
Chambersburg PA
CBHW060000230526
45472CB00008B/1889
9781718762978